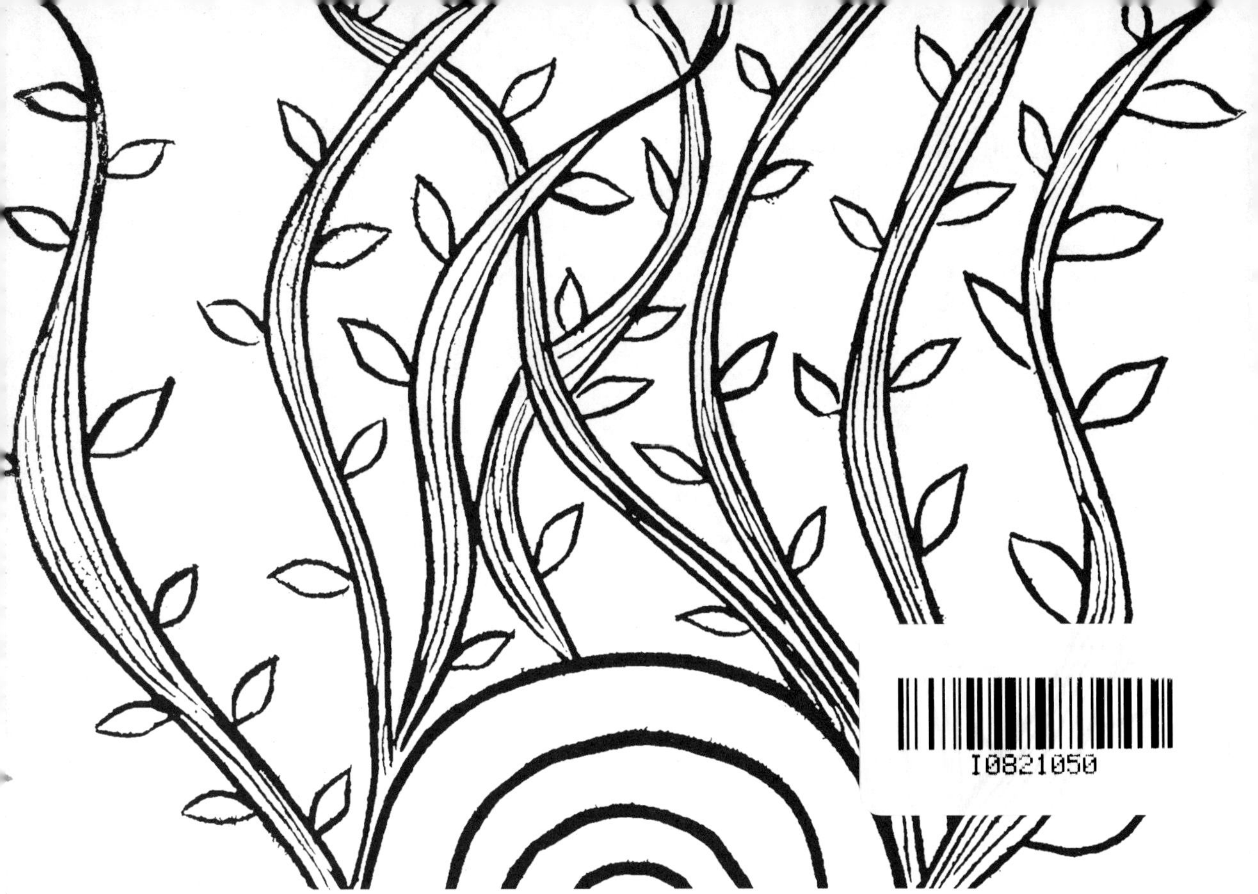

I0821050

ACCESSIBLE ARTS EDUCATION

Principles, Habits, and Strategies to Unleash Every Student's Creativity and Learning

RHODA BERNARD

FOREWORD BY STEPHEN MARK SHORE

Solution Tree | Press

Copyright © 2026 by Solution Tree Press

Materials appearing here are copyrighted. With one exception, all rights are reserved. Readers may reproduce only those pages marked "Reproducible." Otherwise, no part of this book may be reproduced or transmitted in any form or by any means (electronic, photocopying, recording, or otherwise) without prior written permission of the publisher. This book, in whole or in part, may not be included in a large language model, used to train AI, or uploaded into any AI system.

555 North Morton Street
Bloomington, IN 47404
800.733.6786 (toll free) / 812.336.7700
FAX: 812.336.7790

email: info@SolutionTree.com
SolutionTree.com

Visit **go.SolutionTree.com/differentiatedinstruction** to download the free reproducibles in this book.

Printed in the United States of America

Library of Congress Cataloging-in-Publication Data
Names: Bernard, Rhoda (Professor of music education) author
Title: Accessible arts education : principles, habits, and strategies to unleash every student's creativity and learning / Rhoda Bernard.
Description: Bloomington, IN : Solution Tree Press, [2026] | Includes bibliographical references and index.
Identifiers: LCCN 2025009012 (print) | LCCN 2025009013 (ebook) | ISBN 9798893740332 paperback | ISBN 9798893740349 ebook
Subjects: LCSH: Children with disabilities--Education--United States | Arts--Study and teaching--United States
Classification: LCC LC4025 .B47 2026 (print) | LCC LC4025 (ebook)
LC record available at https://lccn.loc.gov/2025009012
LC ebook record available at https://lccn.loc.gov/2025009013

Solution Tree
Cameron L. Rains, CEO
Edmund M. Ackerman, President

Solution Tree Press
Publisher: Kendra Slayton
Associate Publisher: Todd Brakke
Acquisitions Director: Hilary Goff
Editorial Director: Laurel Hecker
Art Director: Rian Anderson
Managing Editor: Sarah Ludwig
Copy Chief: Jessi Finn
Production Editor: Paige Duke
Copy Editor: Anne Marie Watkins
Text and Cover Designer: Fabiana Cochran
Acquisitions Editor: Carol Collins
Content Development Specialist: Amy Rubenstein
Associate Editor: Elijah Oates

To educators—your devotion to learning, your subjects, and your students inspires me every day. I feel privileged to be among your ranks and to learn from and with all of you.

ACKNOWLEDGMENTS

It is not hyperbole to say that writing this book has been the realization of a lifelong dream. I remember first getting to know someone who had written several academic books and feeling driven to find a way, someday, to do the same. It has taken more than thirty years since I met that person for this book to be published.

I am deeply grateful for the many people who have supported me in various ways to make this project possible.

First, there are those who provided me with space, time, and resources. Thank you to Berklee College of Music for granting me my first-ever sabbatical leave so that I could step away from the day-to-day treadmill. Thank you to my Berklee colleagues Dr. Cecil Adderley, Dr. Lenora Helm Hammonds, and Dr. Marcela Castillo-Rama for their encouragement before and during the sabbatical. Thank you to my team at the Berklee Institute for Accessible Arts Education for taking on additional responsibilities and continuing our operations in my absence. Special thanks to administrative team members Oriana Inferrera, Marlene Markard, Daniel Martinez del Campo, and Eliza Shaughnessy for stepping up with thoughtfulness, care, grace, and a sense of humor. Thank you to Berklee's Office of Faculty Development for the Chalk Hill Artist Residency so that I could gather with three delightful colleagues in beautiful Healdsburg, California. Thank you to my dear friend Julie Duty for hosting me for a weeklong writing retreat at her wonderful barn in Arizona.

Then, there are those who contributed in some way to my writing process. Thank you to Carol Collins, my acquisitions editor at Solution Tree Press, whose cold email and warm conversation were the ideal catalysts to bring this book from concept to reality. Thank you to my fellow coworkers for the productive pleasure of our weekly sessions and lunches. A very special thank-you to the "women of courage," Corinne McKamey and Cleti Cervoni, for your insightful feedback and wisdom in response to drafts of literally every word written here.

I'd like to thank my chosen family for their personal support. Thank you to Jeff Wallach, Jocelyn Williams, Carolyn Costle, Tom Tyler (who proclaimed, "Of all the people who say that they're going to write a book, when you say it, Rhoda, I am sure that it's true!"), Monica Bhattacharyya, Jen Harris, David Condon, Ed Perlmutter, Paul Dixon, Rachel Bowman, Laurie Ellington, Jennifer Huth, Joanna Messing, Dom Nicholas, and Gail and Betsy Leondar-Wright. Thank you for surrounding me with love and for being interested in my work (or feigning that interest very convincingly!). I am truly fortunate to have you in my life. Thank you for making this journey with me—it's much better with your company.

Finally, thank you to all the artists who shared their experiences for this book. Here's a bit about each of them in their own words.

- **Adrian Anantawan** is a violinist and educator, the chair of music at Milton Academy, and the artistic director of Shelter Music Boston. He is also an associate professor in the String Department at Berklee College of Music, where he founded the Music Inclusion Ensemble. Adrian performs, teaches, and speaks around the world as an advocate for disability and the arts.

- **Mark Beer** is an actor and director who lives in the United Kingdom. He was born with second-degree cerebral palsy and is a wheelchair user. He has worked professionally for over forty years in theater, film, television, and radio. Mark has toured the United Kingdom and Ireland in a wide variety of character roles. Most recently, Mark has performed in London's West End.
- **Megan Bent** is a visual artist who is drawn to image-making processes that reflect and embrace her disabled experience, especially interdependence, impermanence, care, and slowness. Her work has been exhibited throughout the United States and abroad. She has been an artist in residence in the United States and was a recipient of the Wynn Newhouse Award in 2023.
- **Ella Bouvard** is a para-athlete and musician. Her main sports are triathlon, wheelchair rugby, and rugby. Ella is a self-taught guitarist and singer and often performs at pub shows and summer festivals.
- **Rae Brazill** is a songwriter, designer, and director from Leeds, United Kingdom. As the front person of the alt-rock quartet Artio, they write songs that explore their existence as a whole and that are deeply rooted in their identity as a neurodivergent, queer person, addressing personal and social issues.
- **Jeremy Andrew Davis** is a multihyphenate writer, film director, disability advocate, representation consultant, entrepreneur, and social media content creator. He is on a mission to transform disability representation, shaping the cultures of tomorrow through the stories told today.
- **Grace Tussing Douglas** is a blind musical theater actress and sound designer. Through her art and design, she advocates for disability representation and accessibility in the performing arts.
- **Sophia Grech**, internationally celebrated mezzo-soprano, is based in the United Kingdom. She has received great acclaim for her performances at leading concert halls,

opera houses, and international festivals worldwide, leading to regular invitations to give master classes around the world. In 2015, Sophia was diagnosed with autism, and she is now an appointed ambassador on behalf of associated organizations worldwide alongside her artistic career.

- **Cherylee Houston,** MBE (Member of the Order of the British Empire), is a British actress known for her roles as Izzy Armstrong in *Coronation Street*, Britain's longest-running soap series, and as Maz, a character in the comedy series *Tinsel Girl*. She is a self-professed accidental advocate and activist for deaf, disabled, and neurodivergent artists and works to raise awareness for accessibility issues. At twenty-three, she was diagnosed with hypermobile Ehlers-Danlos syndrome (type 3) and has been a wheelchair user ever since.
- **Shane Lowe** is the percussionist and music director of the bands Midair Decision and The Blues Pilots, as well as for the Latina pop artist Precious Perez. Shane specializes in hand percussion and has led performances at prestigious venues such as the Kennedy Center in Washington, DC, and the Lincoln Center in New York.
- **Ben Lunn** is a composer, conductor, and musicologist based in Scotland. His works have been performed throughout Europe, and he has academic writing published internationally. Ben is a cofounder of the Disabled Artist Network, guest artistic director of Hebrides Ensemble, and associate composer at Drake Music Scotland, and his music is published in Universal Edition.
- **Amy Claire Mills** is a textile artist, curator, and producer from Australia who lives and works on Gadigal and Wangal land. Her practice explores advocacy, identity, and resistance, with a focus on disability culture and its social and political dimensions, engaging both as an artist and subject.

- **Jennifer Msumba** is a Florida-based Boston native, an award-winning musician on the autism spectrum, and an ambassador for the Doug Flutie Jr. Foundation for Autism. Her music mixes folk and acoustic indie-pop elements, with lyrics that take you into her unique world and leave you better for it.
- **Precious Perez** is a blind Puerto Rican singer, songwriter, author, and disability advocate. Her goal is to uplift all the communities she represents by being the first blind Latina at the forefront of the Latinx music industry.
- **Rebecca Faith Quinn** is an autism advocate, actress, and full-time content creator whose projects highlight neurodiversity and disability. She has been recognized as a semifinalist and quarterfinalist in screenwriting competitions.
- **Briana Raucci** is a Connecticut-based film and digital photographer, visual artist, and designer. Diagnosed with cerebral palsy at the age of nine months and epilepsy at age twelve, Briana is passionate about disability advocacy through art.
- **Matthew Raynor** is an avid traveler, commercial fisherman, and photographer who, before his accident, chronicled his time at sea through photography. On April 18, 2019, Matthew suffered a severe spinal injury resulting in paralysis below the collarbone, with no hand movement and limited arm mobility. Despite his disability, Matthew continues to capture the beauty of Mother Nature through drone photography and other means.
- **Finnegan Shannon** is an American multidisciplinary artist based in Brooklyn, New York, whose practice focuses on disability culture in inaccessible spaces. Finnegan is most known for their protest pieces, such as gallery benches criticizing a lack of seating and lounges for those who cannot access stairs.

- **Stephen Tonti** is a native of New Orleans, Louisiana, and an adult ADHD advocate, educator, influencer, and public speaker. When not working in complex mental health, Stephen is a writer and producer for film and television. He is the cofounder of Attention Different, a company dedicated to ADHD advocacy, education, and creative content.
- **Madge Woollard** is a pianist and piano teacher based in the United Kingdom. Diagnosed with autism as an adult, Madge specializes in teaching neurodivergent students.

Solution Tree Press would like to thank the following reviewers:

Sarah Kranz
K–5 Art Educator
New Glarus Elementary School
New Glarus, Wisconsin

Lana Powers
Department Chair for Business, FACS, Fine Arts and Technology
Evansville Central High School
Evansville, Indiana

Jennifer Steele
Assistant Director, Athletics and Activities
Fort Smith Public Schools
Fort Smith, Arkansas

Laurie H. Warner
Founder, Advocate, and Educational Consultant
Beyond the Gray Area, LLC
Anthem, Arizona

Hannah Winsnes
Instructor, School of Arts and Education
Red Deer Polytechnic
Red Deer, Alberta, Canada

Visit **go.SolutionTree.com/differentiatedinstruction** to download the free reproducibles in this book.

TABLE OF CONTENTS

Reproducibles are in italics.

ABOUT THE AUTHOR

Rhoda Bernard, EdD, is an internationally renowned expert in accessible arts education. She is the managing director of the Berklee Institute for Accessible Arts Education and the assistant chair of the Music Education Department at Berklee College of Music. Previously, Dr. Bernard was the chair of the Music Education Department at Boston Conservatory at Berklee. Dr. Bernard regularly presents keynotes and research at conferences throughout the United States and abroad, and she provides professional development workshops for educators in local, national, and international forums. Dr. Bernard has written many book chapters and articles in peer-reviewed journals. She was recently honored with the Irene Buck Service to Arts Education Award from Arts|Learning. A vocalist and pianist who specializes in jazz music and Jewish music in Yiddish and Hebrew, Dr. Bernard performs regularly with a number of klezmer bands and has recorded two CDs with the band Klezamir.

Dr. Bernard holds a bachelor of arts cum laude in government from Harvard University and a bachelor of music with academic honors in jazz voice from the New England Conservatory. She earned both her master of education and doctor of education degrees from the Harvard Graduate School of Education.

To learn more about Dr. Bernard's work, follow **@rhodabernard41** on Instagram and **@rhoda-bernard-075a6710b** on LinkedIn.

To book Rhoda Bernard for professional development, contact **pd@SolutionTree.com**.

FOREWORD

BY STEPHEN MARK SHORE

A long time ago, in a land far, far away—not really, just a few miles away—I was invited to a lawyer's home in Brookline, Massachusetts, to meet a group of people interested in giving music lessons to autistic individuals. It started small with just a few people sharing ideas about teaching autistic individuals to play a musical instrument. "What could be better?" I thought. As an autistic person who studied music education through doctoral-level coursework and who has a studio of autistic music students, I thought this seemed the way to go!

When I was diagnosed as autistic, nonspeaking, and "too sick" for inpatient treatment at two and a half, my parents refuted medical professional recommendations that I be institutionalized. Instead, they chose an intensive home-based early intervention program. Among many strategies they employed, imitation and musical interaction were included. After my parents' attempts to get me to imitate them failed, they flipped it around and imitated me—building a base of connection from which they could then develop a trusting relationship. Meeting the person where they are and building a connection are two critical prerequisites for constructing a trusting relationship from which to develop meaningful interaction to do meaningful work with an individual. I find people who go through these first two steps—be it automatically or from being taught—are best at being with autistic and otherwise neurodivergent people. It's an effective approach with everyone, actually.

Music and the other arts are particularly good at initially connecting with autistic and otherwise neurodivergent individuals because they access a different part of the brain than what is used for verbal communication. Even from my nonspeaking days before the age of four, music was an integral part of my upbringing. Classical and folk music played all day and late into the night in my home. My parents and I would move, do tasks, learn with music—we did everything to music.

At age six, I started piano lessons, from which I learned, most importantly, how *not* to teach autistic or otherwise neurodivergent individuals to play the piano. My early experiences in receiving music lessons drive my mission to contrast with "typical music lesson strategy." One way I do this is to involve my students in developing, and later employing, the materials that will be instrumental in learning notation. While this particular technique was developed for autistic students, it can be generalized to neurotypical students as well. The same is true with the strategies you'll learn in this book.

Accessible Arts Education teaches the concepts of accessible instruction and generalizes them to arts education as a whole. The multitude of strategies in this text transform learning into a highly visual, experiential process in which student and educator cocreate together. Rather than an "I teach and you learn" philosophy, teaching music and the other arts becomes collaborative. This treasure of a book has my highest recommendation and is a must-read for anyone wishing to make fulfilling and productive learning in music and the other arts the rule rather than the exception for autistic and otherwise neurodivergent individuals.

Stephen Mark Shore, EdD, is an internationally known professor, author, presenter, consultant, and autistic individual.

[My professor] was also just really willing to listen. He was one of those teachers who, no matter what I was struggling with, he never dismissed those struggles. He always just sat and listened and would work through it with me. Would process it with me. To get to the root of whatever I was struggling with, so that we could understand it and work on it together. And that was a very safe experience for me as an autistic performer, because it felt like, "Oh, I have a safe space to be autistic in this space. I don't have to pretend like I get it. You'll be OK if I don't get it." And that was so comforting.

—Rebecca Faith Quinn,
autism advocate, actress,
and content creator

INTRODUCTION

When I think back on my years as a public school student in the United States in the 1970s and early 1980s, I remember an education that reflected where thinking and practice in the field were at the time. Specifically, most of my teachers (with a couple notable exceptions) used what I would describe today as a *unidimensional pedagogical process* to teach us concepts, facts, and skills. By this, I mean that they used only one approach, only one set of activities, or only one means of assessment.

For example, we learned the concept of time signatures in music class through the following singular process.

1. The teacher told us that the top number in the time signature represents the number of beats per measure.
2. We wrote that definition in a notebook.
3. The teacher told us that the bottom number in the time signature represents the kind of note that gets one beat.
4. We wrote that definition in a notebook.
5. For homework, we were required to memorize the two definitions.

6. We were asked to write out those definitions on a pencil-and-paper test.

When it comes to learning facts, spelling is a good example. We were taught the correct spelling of words through one—and only one—process.

1. Every Monday, our teacher gave us a weekly list of ten spelling words. The teacher wrote the words on the board.
2. We wrote the words in a notebook.
3. For homework, we were required to memorize how to spell the words.
4. There was a pencil-and-paper test at the end of every week that was always in the same format: The teacher would recite each of that week's spelling words, and we would write them down.

Note-taking is an example of a skill we were taught in a unidimensional way.

1. The teacher sat at the overhead projector and wrote the notes they wanted us to take in a specific format on a transparency. The notes were projected on a screen.
2. We copied the content and formatting of the teacher's notes into a notebook. The copies were required to be exact replicas of the teacher's notes.
3. The teacher collected our notebooks and graded them based on the accuracy of our copying.

These and other unidimensional pedagogical processes throughout my public schooling led to a situation where students who could learn effectively through the particular pedagogical process that was employed and demonstrate what they had learned through the singular form of assessment that was utilized were successful. They were viewed—and came to see themselves—as intelligent, hardworking, "good" students. On the flip side, the students who could not learn effectively through that pedagogical process or demonstrate what they had learned through that form of assessment were not successful. They may have come to understand that they were not learning "correctly." They may have been expected—even required—to alter the way they learn to meet their teachers where they were. They may have come to see themselves as not intelligent, not hardworking, or even "bad" or "lazy" students.

Specifically, related to the preceding examples, my classmates who did not learn effectively by memorizing facts would have experienced great difficulty learning and understanding the concept of time signatures. Individuals who needed more time to process letters would have done poorly on the spelling tests. Students who struggled with pencil-and-paper tasks or had trouble translating their thoughts into writing would have found the tests and note-taking tasks to be extremely challenging.

I was fortunate to be able to learn effectively and show what I had learned and was able to do through the unidimensional pedagogical processes and forms of assessment of my public school education. As a result, my learning was seen, appreciated, and validated; I was a successful student, and I excelled in school. But what about my classmates who were not considered successful students? What was going on for them?

Making Learning Visible

I suspect a large number of my classmates who were not considered successful students *were* actually learning. However, because they weren't learning or demonstrating their learning in the way that aligned with the singular pedagogical processes employed in their classes, their learning was not seen, appreciated, or validated by their teachers. Put another way, I believe these students were learning, but their learning was invisible to most of their teachers.

Learning is an achievement that deserves to be marveled at—it merits acknowledgment, validation, and celebration. It is one of the most awe-inspiring things we do. When we learn, we gain understanding, develop skills, grow knowledge, embrace

perspectives, and think differently. We encounter, synthesize, and assimilate new ideas, new works, new processes, and new activities. Learning is a powerful, mesmerizing endeavor. I, like many of you, became an educator because of my intense wonder at and fascination with learning. I still feel that wonder and fascination every day, after more than thirty years in the field. Learning continues to be fresh and exciting. It hasn't gotten old or stale.

Unfortunately, invisible learning can lead to the mistaken assumption that learning has not occurred at all. Personally, this elicits a strong reaction in me. I find it to be nothing short of tragic when this mistaken assumption takes hold. When I think about the students in my classes back in the 1970s and early 1980s who were actually learning (though the majority of their teachers could not see their learning because it was invisible to them) and about the assumptions teachers made about whether they had learned, whether they could learn, and whether they were "good" students, I am deeply saddened. I also feel angry. Mind you, I am not angry at the teachers; I am angry at the situation. I feel angry that common thinking about education at the time created the conditions for some of my classmates' learning not to be visible to most of their teachers.

Invisible learning is not any person's fault; rather, it is a function of the ways that the educational process and learning are conceptualized and, more specifically, the limitations of those conceptualizations. For example, the invisible learning that took place during my public school education likely stemmed from two main sources: (1) the widely established and agreed-on practice of employing a singular pedagogical process to teach concepts, facts, and skills and (2) the commonly held understanding at the time that it was the student's responsibility to change the way they learn to connect with that pedagogical process.

What I am describing here is, of course, just one sort of instance where learning was invisible to others. There have been, are, and will be many more occasions of invisible learning.

When understandings of the educational process and of learning are limited, it becomes more likely that learning outside of the narrow confines of those understandings will take place. And that learning will end up being invisible.

Thankfully, the fertile ground of the late 1900s and early 2000s in the field of education has cultivated numerous advances that have expanded the ways the educational process is conceptualized and, in turn, have made more learning visible. These include (but are not limited to):

- The theory of multiple intelligences (Gardner, 1983)
- Critical pedagogy (Freire, 1970)
- Teaching for understanding (Blythe, 1998)
- Differentiated instruction (Tomlinson, 1995)
- Universal Design for Learning (UDL; Orkwis & McLane, 1998)
- Culturally sustaining pedagogy (Paris & Alim, 2017)

Today, it is generally acknowledged and understood that people learn in different ways, and the wide range of ways in which people learn requires that teachers engage a multidimensional set of pedagogical processes and utilize multiple forms of assessment. Thanks to this broadened understanding of the processes of teaching and learning, learning is far more visible today than it was back in the 1970s and 1980s. For that, I am grateful. It fuels my mission and gives me hope.

Making learning visible has been the laser focus of my career as an educator, leader, and researcher. I have devoted my professional life to developing and providing arts education opportunities where every person's learning can be seen, heard, acknowledged, celebrated, and marveled at. With like-minded colleagues around the world, I have developed the frameworks and practices of accessible arts education. Accessible arts education seeks to make learning visible by striving to eliminate barriers to student engagement, participation, and learning. Today, these frameworks and practices have been embraced

by educators working in all settings, teaching all subject areas, and working with students of all ages, backgrounds, and learning schemes.

Honoring the Origins of Accessible Arts Education

While accessible arts education is widely relevant and applicable to all subject areas, educational situations, and student populations, its origins lie in the many challenges that arts educators have experienced when working with students with disabilities and diagnoses. Not having received pedagogical training for teaching students with diverse learning strengths, challenges, and needs for support, arts educators have long felt ill-equipped to reach every student. Since the 1990s, my colleagues and I have strived to meet this need by developing tools, frameworks, practices, and habits of mind that can help educators (arts and non-arts alike) to make their teaching more accessible for all students. These efforts are ongoing and generative: Teachers in all settings continue to require additional training, resources, and support when it comes to accessibility, and a growing community of educators and leaders continues to create and disseminate new approaches and materials.

This book honors the origins of accessible arts education in two key ways.

1. By including first-person perspectives and contributions from disabled artists and arts educators
2. By respecting the wishes of the disability community in the language that is used

The following sections look at each of these in greater detail.

First-Person Perspectives

From my very first conception of this book, it has been extremely important to me that people with disabilities are included in the text in meaningful ways. As I explore in more depth in chapter 2 (page 57), the voices of people with disabilities are often absent from publications, events, and conversations that have to do with disability, leading to the unfortunate situation where nondisabled people write about and speak for disabled people.

To address this issue and spotlight the first-person perspectives of people with disabilities, this book features artwork by a disabled artist at the beginning of each chapter, as well as vignettes and quotes by disabled artists and arts educators throughout the text. You can learn more about all of these contributors and their work in their biographies in the book's acknowledgments (page vi). I am deeply grateful to all of these individuals for their generosity, honesty, and vulnerability. Our collaborations have been joyful, fascinating, moving, and productive. I am proud to have gotten to know you and to share your words and your artwork in these pages.

The vignettes were developed through a narrative interview process where I asked each individual open-ended questions about their art and their arts education. I transcribed these interviews in full and analyzed them through a grounded-theory approach, through which I uncovered resonant themes and identified excerpts to propose for inclusion in the book. I shared the proposed excerpts with the interviewees, and we jointly edited them when necessary. Once we finalized the excerpts, the interviewees gave their express permission to include their words in the book.

The process for the creation of the artwork was an iterative one that included several discussions between artist Megan Bent and me about the role of the artwork in relation to the text. I shared materials from the book with Megan, and she constructed drafts of black-and-white prints for my review. Together, we arrived at a consensus about the final pieces that have been included in the book, with her permission.

A Note About Language and Disability

Some of the most common questions I hear from educators have to do with language. They want to know what they should say when speaking about disability or about students with disabilities and diagnoses. They are also anxious to know what they should not say in those instances and what words or phrases they should avoid. They fear making a mistake, saying the wrong thing, and offending someone. Over the years, I have developed—and continue to update—classes, professional development modules, talking points, and resources about language and disability, and I always devote at least a few minutes of every session or workshop that I give to the topic.

Language about disability is complex because it is not static; it is constantly changing. Some words and phrases that were once acceptable are considered offensive today, and it can be very challenging to remain current and ensure that you use language that is appropriate and will not lead to any issues.

When it comes to language, I seek to respect the wishes of the disability community in two main ways. First, I consult the writings and presentations of disability self-advocates for information about language and disability. Two individuals whom I have gotten to know personally, Lydia X. Z. Brown and Emily Ladau, have each created a number of particularly helpful blog posts, presentation videos, and publications. These resources help me stay abreast of evolutions in the language that should be used in relation to disability. Second, I respect the ways that disabled individuals and their families refer to themselves and to their family member with a disability. It is my firm conviction that it is never anyone's place to tell another person how to describe themselves or their family members. People have every right to use whatever language they wish when they speak about themselves or members of their families, even if the language they choose includes words or phrases that disability self-advocates have deemed offensive. I believe it is absolutely essential that we respect other people's rights to represent themselves and their families.

For the purposes of the present book, I would like to address two linguistic approaches that are particularly relevant here: person-first language and identity-first language. When we use person-first language, the word *person* is the first word in the statement, and when we use identity-first language, the disability or diagnosis comes first. Table I.1 presents a few examples of person-first and identity-first language.

TABLE I.1: Person-First and Identity-First Language

Person-First Language	Identity-First Language
Person with a disability	Disabled person
Person who uses a wheelchair	Wheelchair user
Person with dyslexia	Dyslexic person
Person with autism	Autistic person

While person-first language was part of the People First movement of the 1970s and was written into the Americans With Disabilities Act in 1990 and the Individuals With Disabilities Education Act in 1997, there have always been some individuals—often disability self-advocates—who push back against person-first language and strongly prefer identity-first language (Wooldridge, 2023).

The aim of person-first language, initially, was to use a linguistic construction that would minimize the potential stigma of disability. Some individuals and organizations choose to use person-first language for that very reason. However, individuals who prefer identity-first language argue that person-first language serves to minimize their disability. They believe that their disability is integral to who they are; they are not ashamed of it, and they wish to foreground it in how they are described.

My advice is that, whenever possible, we should ask the person what they prefer and respect their wishes. If we are going to speak about one individual or a small group of people, it is feasible to ask them whether we should use person-first or identity-first language. When it comes to a larger group, there may be representatives of that group to whom we can turn for guidance.

My own use of person-first and identity-first language has changed over time. Earlier in my career, I only used person-first language. As the years passed and my work grew and developed, I got to know a number of individuals who rejected person-first language and insisted that I use identity-first language. Today, I deliberately alternate between person-first and identity-first language when I speak and write. In this way, I intend to demonstrate that I understand and value both linguistic conventions and that I seek to include everyone by putting forth both perspectives when I communicate. Throughout this book, as you have already seen, I will use both person-first and identity-first language in my references to people with disabilities or disabled people.

Using This Book

This book will introduce educators to the principles, habits of mind, framework, strategies, and approaches of accessible arts education so they can better reach every learner. Although the materials in this book stem from arts education, they apply to all subject matter, within and beyond the arts. They can be used at all levels, in all educational settings, in all kinds of teaching and learning situations, and with all students, no matter how they learn best.

Chapters include:

- Artwork by a disabled artist
- At least one vignette or quote from a disabled artist or arts educator

- Valuable, cutting-edge information from research and practice about the chapter's topic
- Strategies for educators that can be used in all subject areas, in all educational settings, and with all learners
- Reproducibles for educators to copy and use that support the planning and implementation of accessible arts education strategies

Chapter 1 introduces the principles and habits of mind of accessible arts education and provides what I refer to as *high-percentage teaching strategies* to identify and remove barriers to accessibility. These strategies are easy to implement and have a high likelihood of increasing the accessibility of educational experiences for all students.

Chapter 2 explores issues of power in education and puts forth strategies to encourage students to exercise control and agency in teaching and learning settings. While it can feel risky for educators to relinquish some of their power in their teaching situations, when students experience having control and agency, new learning pathways become possible. This chapter provides some simple ways to encourage student control and agency while still maintaining overall authority and ensuring that students work to meet the learning objectives you have set for them.

Chapter 3 delves into student anxiety as a barrier to learning and outlines strategies to create a safe learning space. Many individuals experience anxiety in school for a wide variety of reasons. Research confirms what we all know from our experience as educators: When students are anxious, they are unable to engage, participate, or learn effectively. The strategies in this chapter can help educators alleviate their students' anxiety so they can feel safe and ready to learn.

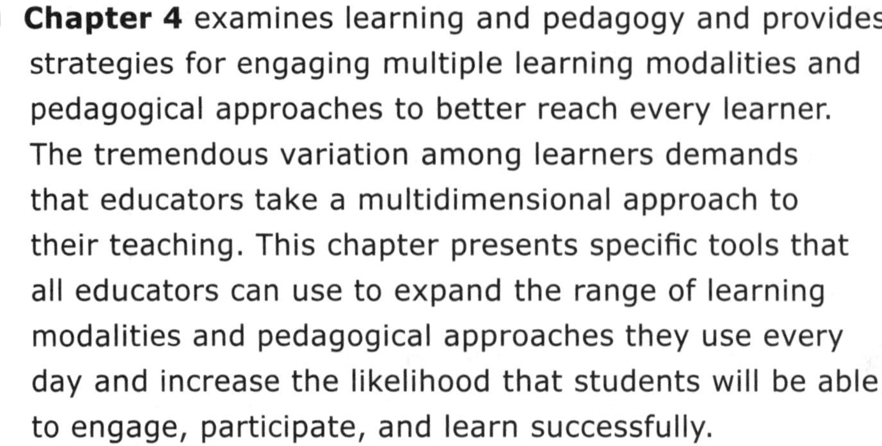

- **Chapter 4** examines learning and pedagogy and provides strategies for engaging multiple learning modalities and pedagogical approaches to better reach every learner. The tremendous variation among learners demands that educators take a multidimensional approach to their teaching. This chapter presents specific tools that all educators can use to expand the range of learning modalities and pedagogical approaches they use every day and increase the likelihood that students will be able to engage, participate, and learn successfully.

- **Chapter 5** narrows in on the unique value of the visual modality and offers strategies to support learning with visual tools. I explore the reasons that the visual modality is the most potent of all the learning modalities, how educators can use the visual modality to its fullest and adapt it for students who are blind or low vision, and what to do in those cases where the visual modality alone may not be effective.

- **Chapter 6** addresses sensory issues that may arise in educational settings and offers strategies to anticipate and alleviate them through careful inventorying, analyzing, and planning, as well as through creating procedures and policies. I share some specific tools that educators can use to modify their learning environment, as well as particular materials that can support students in the moment when sensory issues occur.

- **Chapter 7** focuses on implementation. It features advice for you as you begin your accessible arts education journey, vignettes that illustrate real-world applications of various strategies and tools, and my wishes for you and your students going forward.

Making Learning More Visible

I spend a lot of time with educators, and not just arts educators. In fact, I regularly interact with many educators who teach at all levels, all subject areas, and in all settings. I have been doing so for quite some time—over the course of my career.

In my interactions with educators, it is clear they are dedicated to reaching every student in meaningful ways in all aspects of the educational process. But often, they do not possess the training or support to turn their dedication into action. As a result, they are ravenous for more ways to think about and execute their practice to make it more accessible for every student. Accessible arts education is exactly what they need to satisfy their hunger. After they have studied accessible arts education in some way—through a workshop, course, study group, or conference—teachers often contact me to share some of the ways that implementing these strategies and approaches has transformed their teaching for the better. I also hear from teachers who are excited to share how they have utilized what they learned from these principles and practices to develop their own strategies for particular students or situations.

The field of education is vibrant and generative in ways that give me great hope when it comes to making learning more visible. Thanks to the principles, habits of mind, and pedagogical strategies of accessible arts education, today's educators—no matter the setting or subject area—are better equipped than ever to see, recognize, marvel at, and celebrate every student's learning. As a result, learning is becoming more visible for more students every day.

In the Artist's Words

I think [my poetry teacher] was the first one to use the word *potential* in a non-stinging way. Right, so like other people would be like, "Oh, you have so much potential if you could just . . ." Right? "Stop making excuses, Tonti, you have so much potential." [My poetry teacher] was the first one to go, "In you, I see so much potential, and I am thrilled to see where it goes." That's why—her explanation for paying attention to me was, "You have so much potential I'm thrilled by it. . . . What excites me about you is the potential to burst." And I was like, "Oh—positive attention!" (S. Tonti, personal communication, September 17, 2024)

—**Stephen Tonti**, ADHD coach and influencer, public speaker, and writer and producer for film and television

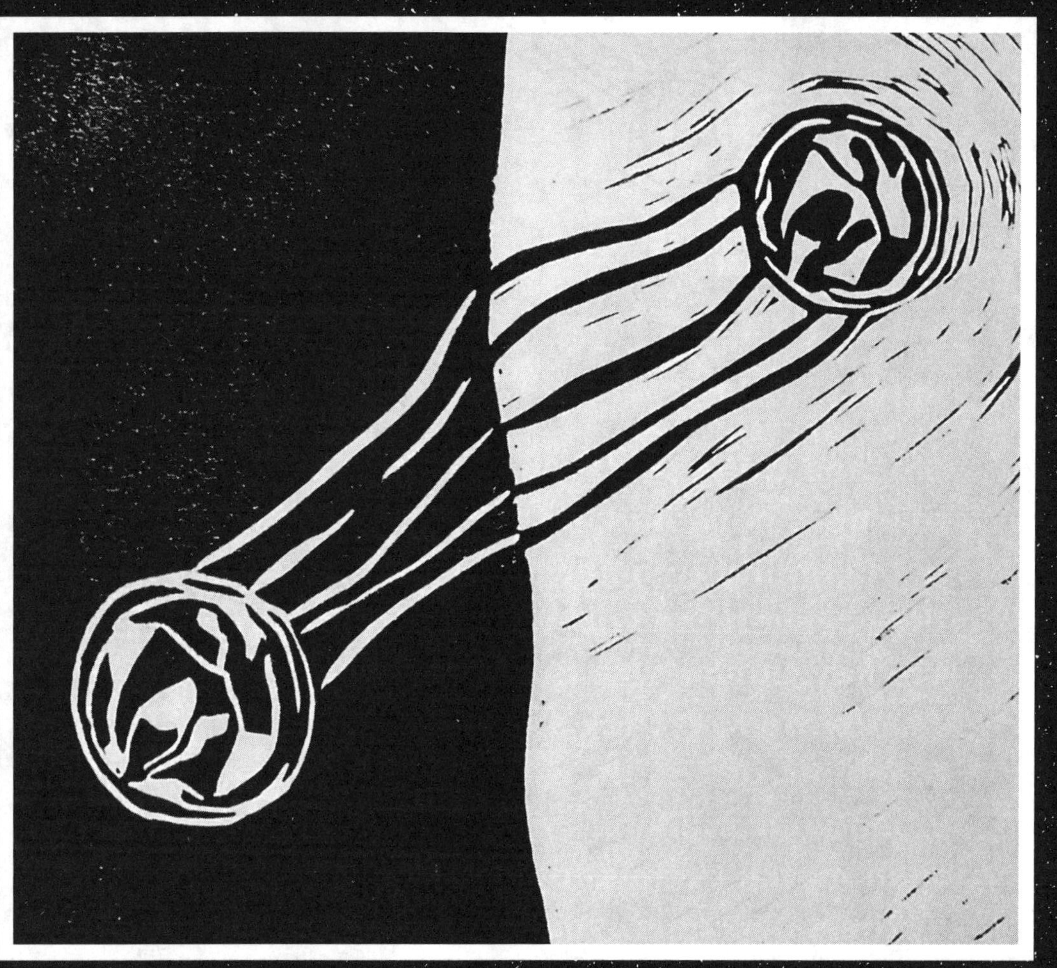

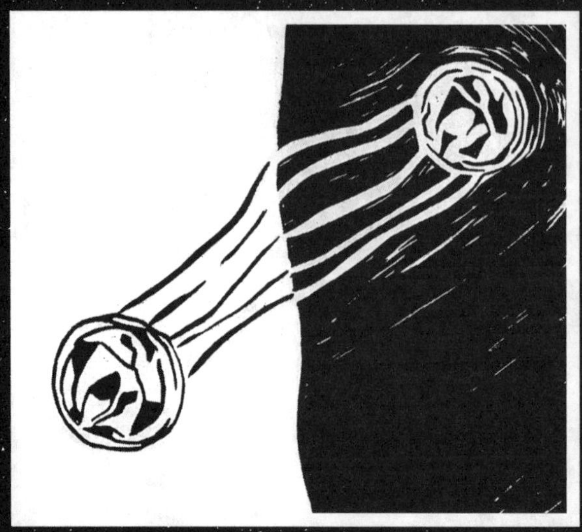

The one thing pretty much all of my one-to-one teachers have had, be it brass or composition, is the ability to go at the pace of the person they're working with. I think that is really the key thing more than anything else. . . . That's the real trick and difficulty, I think, of teaching, generally, is to go at the pace that, when your student's going well, you need to then match them and not slow them down, but at the same time, you don't want to always be demanding that they do things quickly, because sometimes they need just a smidgen more time just to make sense of it, and then can go on and do.

—Ben Lunn, composer, conductor, and founder of the Disabled Artist Network

CHAPTER 1
INTRODUCING ACCESSIBLE ARTS EDUCATION

My work in accessible arts education began in the mid-1990s in my earliest days and years as an educator, when I was a new college faculty member teaching music theory and sight singing courses at a prestigious music conservatory where I had also been a student. I was enraptured with teaching, and I was fascinated by learning. My students intrigued and captivated me. I strived to get to know each of them as individuals, in my class, in the hallways, and on the streets of our urban campus. I sought to understand how each person learns and thinks so I could promote and facilitate their growth. Unbeknownst to me then, I was already engaging accessible arts education principles, habits of mind, and practices—I just didn't have the context or the vocabulary to conceive of my teaching in terms of accessible arts education. That context and vocabulary had not yet emerged in the fields of education, special education, and arts education.

Back then, I taught several sections of a four-course sequence of extremely rigorous, required sight singing and music theory courses. Every student in the institution took all four courses, and many of the students struggled. Each semester, a few dozen students failed the courses and were required to retake them the following semester. To accommodate those students, the department created special sections of the courses, known as the remedial sections, just for the students who failed the courses the first time around.

In collegiate music programs, sight singing and music theory courses often function as "gatekeeping" courses: Passing those courses is a prerequisite for other coursework and, therefore, for making progress toward the degree. The courses also hold particular significance when it comes to students' identities. By the time a student enrolls as a music performance major at the college level, they have experienced success as a musician and are likely to think of themselves as a musician. For a number of these students, their struggles in the sight singing and music theory course sequence challenge their confidence, their sense of who they are, and their thoughts about their careers. The stakes of these courses, then, are quite high in more than one way.

In my first semester on the faculty, I was assigned to teach the remedial sections of all four courses. I discovered they were my favorite classes to teach. As I got to know my students, I delved deeply into each person's thinking and learning to uncover where the issues might lie. Where were the disconnects in their understanding? Where were the gaps in their skills? How could I bridge the disconnects and gaps in ways that would make sense to them? What kinds of support did they need from me so that they could achieve and succeed?

Teaching the remedial sections was invigorating for me. I was jazzed about the work every day. I couldn't wait to find and address the issues and obstacles that my students were experiencing and to witness their growth and the accomplishments that would follow. And I saw positive results: Over the years, all of my students ended up doing very well in my class, and all of them successfully resumed the sequence of required courses the following semester.

At the same time, my students became more confident. Having begun our class feeling embarrassed and defeated because they had failed the course the previous semester, these young musicians needed something more than a second time through the course material. They needed to see themselves as capable, knowledgeable, talented, and worthy of a conservatory education—perhaps again, perhaps for the very first time. I considered this an important part of my responsibility to my students: not just to help them learn and grow in terms of their knowledge and skills but also to help them rebuild their injured confidence in themselves as students and as musicians.

I could fill an entire book of these students' stories, but for the purpose of this chapter, I will share one representative example.

A young man studying African percussion was struggling with sight singing. It was clear from his participation in class that he understood the music theory concepts and knew what he wanted to sing, but something obstructed his ability to produce the actual sounds with his voice. The student thought there might be a physical issue at play, and he came to my office hours with questions about vocal technique. First, I asked him to sing a familiar song; I wanted to see what would happen when he tried to sing. The student sang a short folk song clearly and accurately. This signaled to me that his challenges with sight singing were not related to the physical aspects of vocal production; rather, there was some other obstacle to his ability to sight-sing correctly.

Next, I asked the student to try some pitch matching exercises. I played a note on the piano and asked him to sing the same note. I tried this several times, with different notes, and the result was the same: The student sang an incorrect note, and he was unable to find the correct note and sing it. As we discussed what it was like for him to try to match the pitches on the piano with his voice, I learned that he had never matched a pitch with his voice before. All of his prior musical experience had been with instrumental music in a non-Western culture. He didn't know how to go about vocal pitch matching.

It seemed that pitch matching was the source of at least some of the student's difficulties with sight singing. In that session, and over the next several weeks, we isolated the skill of pitch matching and pulled it apart from several angles. We strengthened his internal musical ear with ear-training exercises so he could hear pitches in his head before singing them (what is commonly referred to as *audiation* in music education circles). We worked on instrumental pitch matching first, where he would use an instrument to play the same pitch I played on another instrument. Then we turned to vocal pitch matching in different contexts—using his voice to match the pitch from an instrument, from a recording, and from my singing voice—and we developed a series of strategies for him to use. We talked about the sensations related to vocal pitch matching: what it feels like when pitches match and when they do not. Over time, the student's ability to match pitch improved to the point where he could do so easily, consistently, and correctly.

Gaining the skill of vocal pitch matching unlocked a dramatic improvement in the student's sight singing skills, and he could use his voice more reliably to represent his understanding of music theory by singing the pitches he wanted to sing. By the end of the semester, he was able to pass my class and rejoin the sight singing and music theory course sequence.

I didn't know it at the time, but as I was teaching the remedial sections, I was actually engaging in some key practices of accessible arts education, such as the following.

- Striving to understand my students' thinking
- Seeking barriers that might be interrupting or diminishing students' learning and growth
- Devising strategies and approaches to reduce or remove the barriers and promote student success
- Celebrating my students' progress and highlighting what they could do with an asset-based attitude, rather than focusing on issues and challenges through a deficit-based lens

Back then, there was no such thing as accessible arts education—it did not yet exist. Today, accessible arts education is a generative educational framework that educators who teach students of all ages, in all subject areas, and in all educational settings can study and implement.

In the Artist's Words

I took some classes previously in a college setting that involved dance and they were not quite as welcoming to figuring out a way to teach me, because I stay in the front of the class, and that's how I am able to make out some of the teacher's movements. And you also have to communicate with them, "Hey, I need you to be as verbal as possible and you might have to give me some corrections because there's a good chance that I'll interpret something wrong." And there's just been experiences in the past where I was put in a corner and had to do the exact same moves for like half a semester because the teacher just didn't know what to do with me. But here at my university, we have two excellent professors in dance right now, they both have been wonderful with finding different ways to teach me, because it is different and because it has been different my entire life, I'm honestly behind and so, they've been really wonderful of communicating and asking, "Hey! Is this OK if we try things this way for a while or try to problem-solve one way or another?" (Everett, 2023)

—**Grace Tussing Douglas**, blind musical theater actress and sound designer

This chapter explains what accessible arts education is and introduces readers to its key principles and habits of mind. It also features some of accessible arts education's signature pedagogical strategies. I explore many more strategies in subsequent chapters.

Accessible Arts Education Defined

Accessible arts education is a dynamic set of principles, habits of mind, and pedagogical strategies that help educators strive to reach every student, regardless of their strengths, challenges, needs for support, or learning schemes. It is an educational framework for creating and facilitating classes, lessons, and studios that support the learning and growth of every student. Through the synthesis and transformation of the evidence-based practices and resources of arts education, special education, and general education, this approach seeks to break down the silos between disciplines so that educators can reduce and remove barriers that interfere with student engagement, participation, and learning. The resultant educational framework is not fixed; rather, it is a generative approach that educators can use to cultivate the inclusiveness and accessibility of their teaching.

Arts educators receive very little preservice training or in-service support in how to teach students who learn differently, even as they face more and more student diversity in many ways, including how their students learn best (Bernard, 2023; Hourigan, 2007). These conditions have led arts educators, first informally and then more systematically, to develop both the field and the educational framework of accessible arts education with the hope of providing arts educators with tools to reach every student. Let's take a look at the history and development of accessible arts education through three frames: (1) legislation, (2) organizations, and (3) individuals.

The legislative roots of accessible arts education date back to 1963, when President John F. Kennedy signed the Maternal and Child Health and Mental Retardation Planning Amendments to the Social Security Act (John F. Kennedy Presidential Library and Museum, n.d.), which provided funding for research about—as well as treatment, support, and education for—individuals with intellectual disabilities. The 1970s was a pivotal decade of legislative activity related to people with disabilities and accessibility.
The Rehabilitation Act of 1973 prohibits organizations that receive federal funding, including schools, from discriminating on the basis of disability (U.S. Department of Labor, n.d.). The Rehab Act, as it is known, includes Section 504, which requires that federally funded schools provide a free appropriate public education (FAPE) to all disabled students in the school district (U.S. Department of Education, n.d.). The Education for All Handicapped Children Act, passed in 1975 and renamed in 1990 to the Individuals With Disabilities Education Act, supports states in meeting the needs of people with disabilities in educational settings through the

Individualized Education Program (IEP) process of evaluation, accommodations, and special education services (U.S. Department of Education, 2024). The Rehabilitation Act of 1973 and the Individuals With Disabilities Education Act (2004) remain the most significant pieces of legislation relating to accessibility for—and nondiscrimination toward—students with disabilities in U.S. schools.

The history of organizations whose work is related to arts education for people with disabilities also begins with a connection to the Kennedy family. In 1974, ambassador Jean Kennedy Smith created VSA (originally known as Very Special Arts and currently named Access/VSA International Network), an international organization focused on arts, education, and disability that is based at the Kennedy Center (Kennedy Center, n.d.). In the 1990s, VSA led the way in the formal development of accessible arts education by offering the Intersections conference, publishing resources, and presenting professional development workshops (Kennedy Center, n.d.). Soon thereafter, established national arts organizations developed special interest groups dedicated to arts education for people with disabilities as a means of support and networking for educators (American Alliance for Theatre & Education, n.d.; Fehr, 2015; National Art Education Association, 2024). This laid the groundwork for the creation of new organizations in the field of accessible arts education, such as the 2007 launch of the Berklee Institute for Accessible Arts Education, which I founded and direct. The Berklee Institute for Accessible Arts Education provides arts education programs for people with disabilities, graduate programs, and professional development offerings (Berklee College of Music, n.d.).

The following are some of the scholars and practitioners who were influential in the development of accessible arts education in the 1990s and early 2000s.

- Mary Adamek (Iowa School of Music, n.d.)
- Alice Hammel (Dr. Alice Hammel, n.d.)
- Alice-Ann Darrow (Florida State University School of Music, n.d.)
- Juliann Dorff (Kent State University, 2022)

- Lynne Horoschak (Moore College of Art and Design, 2019)
- Judith Jellison (Butler School of Music, n.d.)
- Beverley H. Johns (BevJohns, n.d.)
- Elise Sobol (NYU Steinhardt, n.d.)
- Janet Whitman Knighten (Division of Visual and Performing Arts Education, 2023)

Their early publications and leadership form the foundation of the field. In the ensuing years, numerous others—including myself—have proudly joined their ranks, striving to advance research and practice and nurture the community.

Accessible arts education, both as a field and as an educational framework, is on the rise. Since the early 2000s, we have seen an increasing number of conferences, conventions, publications, courses, and workshops being provided by an expanding cadre of organizations, scholars, and practitioners. Educators all over the world are creating strategies and documenting and sharing them with each other. Since the 2010s, these approaches have extended beyond the arts into other subject areas. Educators in non-arts disciplines have taken notice of these practical strategies to reach every student and have begun to incorporate them into their teaching settings, as well.

It is a very exciting time. And it is the ideal time for this book: the first text to lay out a framework for accessible arts education and provide strategies that every educator can employ with every student in every setting and in every discipline.

Principles of Accessible Arts Education

Three core principles undergird accessible arts education and guide the work of educators in the classroom and researchers in the field. Together, they provide a philosophical grounding for accessible arts education. They also articulate just a few of the ways accessible arts education is expansive: in terms of student population, subject area, and position in the educational process.

Principle 1: Necessary for Some and Helpful for All

Accessible arts education is for *every* student—not just for students with disabilities or diagnoses. Its principles, habits of mind, and pedagogical strategies benefit *all* students. Students need not have a formal diagnosis or a documented disability to benefit from strategies that increase the accessibility of teaching and learning. Educators need not have access to IEP documents about their students for accessible arts education to make a meaningful difference in their teaching.

Rather, accessible arts education is necessary for some students and helpful for all students, to employ a phrase that is often used by the special education community (Bernard, 2023). To elaborate, the strategies and approaches of accessible arts education are "necessary for those students who otherwise would not be able to access the curriculum and the activities. At the same time, they are helpful for all students because they increase that access for everyone" (Bernard, 2023, p. 6).

Many educators who have incorporated accessible arts education into their teaching practice have told me that doing so has had a profoundly positive impact on the effectiveness of their teaching with all their students.

Principle 2: Broadly Applicable, Within and Beyond the Arts

The pedagogical strategies of accessible arts education can be engaged everywhere that teaching and learning occur—within and beyond the arts. Although it originated in the arts, accessible arts education applies to all subject areas, all student populations, all age ranges, and all teaching and learning contexts. While this book is written from the arts education perspective, every strategy and example herein can easily be incorporated into any educational context and any subject area, either as is or with just a few simple tweaks. As a further guide for educators in other subject areas, examples throughout the book will feature applications of accessible arts education approaches to non-arts settings.

Principle 3: Accessible From the Outset

Accessible arts education is a critical and core component of the entire educational process, from planning to teaching, to assessing. It is *not* an add-on—it is not accommodations that are an afterthought, executed once the lesson has already been planned.

When teachers begin by attending to accessibility, they can make a meaningful difference right away—first by anticipating barriers to student engagement, participation, and learning and then by striving to reduce and remove those barriers from the very start. This sets up the educational experience to be more accessible for everyone, leading to fewer surprises or issues that would require adjustments along the way.

On a recent Thursday afternoon, one of my undergraduate students, whom I'll call Louisa, bounded into the classroom, slammed her notebook on her desk, and exclaimed, "I don't get it!" When I asked her what she meant, Louisa replied, "Why is it that, in my other classes, we write out lesson plans, and then we add the accessibility section at the end? Shouldn't we plan our lessons to make them accessible from the very beginning?"

Habits of Mind

Accessible arts education challenges educators to engage new ways of thinking about the educational enterprise. It promotes broader conceptions of learning, student engagement, and teaching. The following three habits of mind and their accompanying questions demonstrate the expansiveness of this approach when it comes to what learning, student engagement, and teaching look like.

Habit of Mind 1: Cultivate a Broad Conception of Learning

Every person learns in their own way, regardless of whether they have a disability or a diagnosis. The wide variability in how people learn is at the core of accessible arts education. Its principles challenge educators to expand their conception of what learning looks like so they can facilitate and discover their students' learning in as many ways as possible. Cultivating a broad conception of learning compels educators to ask, "In what ways is learning taking place?"

Accessible arts education requires teachers to abandon their assumptions of what learning looks like and recognize that learning might be happening in ways that lie beyond the conventional—beyond how they themselves and their students may have learned over the years. That recognition propels teachers to become investigators and instigators of their students' learning, actively seeking to uncover evidence of learning and create multiple, wide-ranging opportunities for their students to demonstrate what they have learned.

Cultivating a broad conception of learning compels educators to ask, "In what ways is learning taking place?"

Several years ago, one of my faculty colleagues reached out to me. She told me about a student in one of her ear-training classes who happened to be on the autism spectrum. This student, according to my colleague, was in serious danger of failing the class because he had not been able to pass a single ear-training test. She went on to say that the student "obviously was not studying," and she didn't know what to do to help him.

In her account, my colleague made a couple of assumptions based on the student's performance: that he had not learned what he needed to learn in the class, and he was not studying.

I can understand why she made these assumptions. They are rooted in a more traditional way of thinking about learning, as I discussed in the introduction (page 1): that learning and assessment take place through a unidimensional pedagogical process. When a pedagogical process is unidimensional, only those students who learn effectively and can demonstrate what they have learned and are able to do effectively through that particular process are successful. Other students—who may very well have learned and grown—are not able to succeed.

Accessible arts education interrupts the train of thought that leads to these sorts of assumptions. By cultivating a broad conception of learning and asking, "In what ways is learning taking place?" educators can approach situations like the one my colleague described as opportunities to investigate the particular student's learning, reveal possible barriers to that learning, and discover ways to reduce or remove those barriers.

As the conversation with my colleague continued, the question "In what ways is learning taking place?" was at the forefront of my mind. To delve into this more, I asked my colleague a question, even though I already knew the answer: "How do you give your ear-training tests?" (I have taken and given dozens of ear-training tests, and they have always taken the same form: The teacher plays a musical excerpt on an instrument, and the student writes what they hear using musical notation.) And that was my colleague's answer. She said, "I play something on the piano, and the students write it down."

I started to wonder whether the use of pencil and paper in the ear-training tests might be a barrier for this student and his learning. Perhaps he possessed the knowledge but was not able to communicate it by writing it down. To investigate this hunch, and to try to get a better sense of the student's learning, I asked my colleague to try an experiment with the student in a one-to-one office hours session. I suggested that she create manipulatives for the student to use (rather than pencil and paper) by drawing a large grand staff on a big piece of construction paper, printing out musical notes of various values, and cutting up the paper so that each musical note was on its own little piece of paper. Then, I suggested that she play some examples for the student in her office and task the student with arranging the little pieces of paper with the notes on them on the construction-paper staff to communicate what he heard her play.

She called me right after the office hours session to report that the student had gotten every example correct when he used the manipulatives!

This experiment confirmed that the student was, in fact, learning, and he had developed his ear-training skills. He could hear and understand the music very well. The pencil-and-paper aspects of the ear-training tests functioned as a barrier that prevented him from showing what he knew. With this newfound knowledge about her student and his learning, my colleague allowed the student to use manipulatives during his ear-training tests for the remainder of the semester. She also collaborated with our Accessibility Resources for Students office to ensure that he received support from an occupational therapist to help him with pencil-and-paper tasks.

Habit of Mind 2: Cultivate a Broad Conception of Student Engagement

Traditionally, in Western cultures, student engagement has been narrowly conceived. Specifically, teachers consider students to be engaged when they are sitting still, refraining from speaking or making any other sounds, and looking at the teacher. We now know that students, regardless of whether they have a disability or a diagnosis, actually engage in a much wider range of ways. As just a couple of examples, some people more effectively pay attention when they look to the side or close their eyes, limiting their visual sensory input; others find that standing and moving their bodies help them be more involved in learning activities. Accessible arts education challenges educators to expand their conception of what student engagement looks like so they can facilitate and spark their students' engagement in as many ways as possible.

Cultivating a broad conception of student engagement compels educators to ask, "What can student engagement look like?"

Several years ago, on the first day of classes, one of my freshman students approached me to discuss the way that she engages best. She told me that she does her best learning when she is doodling: "To look at me, you'd think I'm not paying attention. I'm looking at my paper and the doodles. But, actually, I'm hearing everything. I'm more involved in what's going on in class if I doodle." I gave her permission to doodle during class, and this student was consistently one of the most engaged and motivated students in the group. She regularly contributed to discussions, and she participated fully in every activity—doodling all the while.

Habit of Mind 3: Cultivate a Broad Conception of Teaching

As you read in the introduction (page 1), the wide variability in how people learn demands that educators provide information, facilitate experiences and activities, give feedback, ask questions, and more—that is, teach—in as many ways as possible. Accessible arts education challenges educators to expand their conception of what teaching looks like so they can reach every student, no matter how they learn best. Cultivating a broad conception of teaching compels educators to ask, "What can teaching look like?"

Rather than merely teaching the way they were taught, educators who engage the habits of mind of accessible arts education investigate, explore, create, and improvise as they teach, always seeking to connect with their students and the widely diverse ways in which they learn.

Cultivating a broad conception of teaching compels educators to ask, "What can teaching look like?"

Jane Sapp provides one of the most powerful descriptions of teaching I have ever heard. A music educator in the Springfield, Massachusetts, public schools, Sapp is the subject of the 2002 documentary *Someone Sang for Me: A Portrait of Educator Jane Sapp* by Julie Akeret. In the film, Sapp uses the metaphor of a treasure hunt to describe her approach to teaching:

> What you're trying to do is dig. It's like a treasure. It's like going on a treasure hunt. So the map says maybe it's here. So you dig there. It's not there. But you're determined to find that

> treasure, right? So you say, "Well, I'm going to go over here. I'm going to dig here." And I said, "Well, maybe I should change the tools. Maybe instead of a shovel, I should use a pick." And so now I use this and see if I can find the treasure. Well, that's how we have to see these kids. They are treasures. They are treasures. . . . We, as adults, our role is to find the treasure and then hold it up for them and let them see.

Accessible arts education does not seek to standardize students so they all learn in the same way, nor does it aim to standardize the process of teaching so educators teach using a single pedagogical approach. Rather, finding the treasures—acknowledging, knowing, seeing, validating, and celebrating the uniqueness of each student and how they learn—and using whatever methods it takes to reach them are the goals of accessible arts education practice.

Accessible Arts Education Strategies

Educational experiences are more accessible for all students when there are fewer barriers that interrupt or impede those experiences. Accessible arts education strategies center on anticipating and minimizing barriers to student engagement, participation, and learning. The first step to making educational experiences more accessible to all students takes place during the planning process.

Step 1: Anticipate Barriers by Identifying Them at the Outset

The first step of accessible arts education practice takes place when educators begin designing lessons, activities, assignments, and assessments. As the planning process gets underway, teachers identify any barriers that could interrupt or inhibit student engagement, participation, or learning. A teacher must first know what the barriers are (or could be) to engage accessible arts education strategies to reduce or remove the barriers.

Barriers can exist in all aspects of teaching and learning, including the following.

- **How teachers engage students:** For example, activating prior knowledge can be a barrier if a student does not possess that prior knowledge. Speaking about the work of a particular artist or referring to a book can be a barrier if a student is not familiar with the artist's work or has not read the book.
- **How teachers provide information for students:** For example, communicating information and giving instructions by speaking them can be barriers if a student needs additional time to process auditory information.
- **How teachers require students to participate in activities and assignments:** For example, a group activity can be a barrier if a student is not comfortable interacting with their peers. Requiring students to write an essay can be a barrier if it is difficult for a student to put their thoughts into writing.
- **How teachers assess student learning:** For example, using playing, singing, dancing, or drawing as an assessment can be a barrier if a student's understanding is greater than their ability to demonstrate or perform. Assessing student learning in mathematics class based on how quickly a student can complete a worksheet with multiplication problems can be a barrier if a student needs more time to process written language and numbers.
- **How teachers define progress:** For example, equating progress with steady improvement in skills every week can be a barrier for a student whose perfectionism or anxiety inhibits their ability to execute new skills. In these situations, it might appear at first glance that the student is not making progress when, in fact, they are—it's just that the progress cannot be seen in their execution of the skill. They might have made progress in relation to other aspects of the skill, such as their ability to explain it or detect errors when others perform the skill.

Figure 1.1 shows how a teacher might identify potential barriers to student learning.

Once educators have identified possible barriers that might emerge, they can try to minimize them as they plan lessons, activities, assignments, and assessments. Figure 1.2 (page 34) shows one way teachers could plan strategies to reduce barriers they've identified during their planning process.

Aspect of Pedagogy	Planned Strategy	Possible Barriers
Engage Students	Provide student choice through a class vote.	The class vote will not be every student's first choice, and some students will be unhappy with the result.
Provide Information for Students	Distribute handouts with terms and definitions.	Some students require additional time to process written information. Some students understand symbols more easily than words. Some students find it challenging when there is a large amount of text on a page.
Require Students to Participate	Assign students to work in pairs.	Some students have difficulties interacting with peers and collaborating on assignments because they don't know what to say or how to go about the work.
Assess Student Learning	Use a pencil-and-paper task to gauge student learning.	Some students have difficulties with the physical act of writing. Some students find it challenging to put their thoughts on paper.
Define Progress	Require that students reach particular levels of skill proficiency at midyear and at the end of the year.	Some students may make progress but may not be able to demonstrate it through their skill level.

FIGURE 1.1: Identifying potential barriers.

*Visit **go.SolutionTree.com/differentiatedinstruction** for a free reproducible version of this figure.*

Barrier	Whom It Could Affect	What It Interrupts or Inhibits	Examples of Teaching Strategies to Reduce or Remove the Barrier
Reference to an artist's work or to a book	Student who is unfamiliar with the artist or the book	Student engagement	Introduce the whole class to the artist's work or the book.
Spoken information or instructions	Student who needs additional processing time for auditory input	Student engagement, participation, and learning	Engage visual tools for communicating information or instructions. Use text, symbols, and pictures.
Group activities	Student who is not comfortable with peer interactions	Student participation and learning	Structure the group activities by assigning each student a role, providing the groups with a sequential checklist for their work, and sharing scripts (sentence starters and specific suggestions of things to say in the group). Allow students to complete the activities either individually or in pairs, for those who wish to do so.
Essay writing	Student who has difficulty putting thoughts into writing	Student participation and learning	Engage text-to-speech tools for students who prefer to speak their thoughts. Use graphic organizers to help students think through their ideas and how they are related. Divide the class into pairs who collaborate on the essay and support each other.

			Provide additional choices for students as to what they can produce for the assignment, including videos, PowerPoint presentations, artistic creations, and so on, with clear guidelines for the required elements of the assignment and a rubric for how it will be assessed.
Assessment through demonstration or arts-based performance	Student whose understanding is greater than their ability to perform	Student participation and learning	Assess through additional means, such as by asking students to detect errors in a performance, teach another student the important concepts or elements of the skill, and explain what they know in a presentation or video.
Assessment based on timed tasks	Student who needs additional processing time	Student participation and learning	Allow students to complete the tasks without being timed. Isolate certain portions of the tasks for the students to complete while being timed, and rehearse those tasks with the students to prepare them.
Progress that's defined as steady skill improvement every week	Student whose perfectionism or anxiety inhibits their ability to execute new skills	Student learning	First, abandon this definition of progress. Progress looks different for every learner, and expecting steady improvement every week is unrealistic and unfair. Seek other ways to determine whether students' skills have improved. Ask students to perform the skills in a different modality (to clap instead of play or to move their hands instead of their whole bodies, for example).

FIGURE 1.2: Examining barriers and planning strategies to reduce or remove them.

*Visit **go.SolutionTree.com/differentiatedinstruction** for a free reproducible version of this figure.*

Identifying and anticipating barriers at the outset of the planning process sets the stage for teachers to strive to reduce or remove barriers. That takes us to the next step.

Step 2: Strive to Remove Barriers

After identifying potential barriers to student engagement, participation, and learning, the next step is to strive to reduce or remove them. There are many strategies that educators can employ to minimize barriers and thereby maximize the accessibility of the educational experiences they facilitate. In this section, I discuss five of the most broadly applicable and effective pedagogical strategies in accessible arts education. We'll explore more strategies in subsequent chapters.

I often refer to the following five strategies as *high-percentage teaching strategies*. My use of this phrase stems from a basketball metaphor. In professional and collegiate basketball, statisticians track many aspects of the game, including something called *high-percentage shots*, or shots that, statistically, for a given player, have a high likelihood of going into the basket and therefore being successful. Statisticians track and analyze the relationship between two elements: (1) the player's physical location on the basketball court when they release the ball for the shot and (2) the percentage of the player's shots from that location that go into the basket. For just two examples, some players shoot free throws really well, and those would be high-percentage shots for them; likewise, players with high-percentage shots from the three-point range have great success from behind the three-point line. Coaches use statistics regarding various players and their high-percentage shots to craft plays and forge defensive strategies.

Just as high-percentage shots in basketball have a high likelihood of landing in the basket, high-percentage teaching strategies have a high likelihood of making educational experiences accessible for every student. Educators who incorporate high-percentage teaching strategies into their practice open up myriad pathways for learning for all of their students; the strategies are extremely effective at reducing and removing barriers and, therefore, increase the accessibility of educational experiences for every student.

SPOTLIGHT: DIFFERENTIATED INSTRUCTION

Differentiated instruction is an educational approach that emphasizes tailoring instruction for individual students. It is said that the basic ideas behind differentiated instruction date back to the earliest days of schooling in the United States, where many students at different levels were educated in the same room (Tomlinson, 2014). Since her highly influential 1995 text, *How to Differentiate Instruction in Mixed-Ability Classrooms*, educator Carol Ann Tomlinson has led the way in research and practice when it comes to differentiated instruction. She has published numerous books and articles that develop the concept further and provide educators with practical resources and procedures. According to Tomlinson (2014, 2017), effective differentiation takes place when educators alter and adjust one or more of the following three elements.

1. **Content:** What they learn (knowledge and skills)
2. **Process:** How they learn (activities)
3. **Products:** How they demonstrate their learning (assessments)

The understanding that all people learn differently—often referred to as *learner variability* (Pape, 2018)—undergirds differentiated instruction. Educators who attend to that variability and customize their instruction for it are more likely to create the conditions for effective learning on the part of every student.

STRATEGY 1: SEPARATE THE GOAL FROM THE MEANS

One very effective strategy that educators can engage to eliminate potential barriers is to prioritize their goals for their students without demanding a particular means for reaching those goals.

When the means is embedded within the goal, our teaching becomes less accessible because the means can act as a barrier for some students. When we disentangle the goal and the means, the means becomes flexible and the barrier is reduced. Educator and noted UDL presenter and author Liz Byron uses the phrase "clear goal with flexible means" in a 2019 podcast episode with Tim Bogatz to encourage teachers to engage this strategy. Carol Ann Tomlinson (2014, 2017) refers to this strategy as "creating multiple paths for learning" in a 1997 video.

Two of the previous examples involve goals with the means embedded within them (see figure 1.3).

Goal With Means Embedded	Means or Potential Barrier	Goal With Flexible Means
Learn a concept through a group activity.	Group activity	Learn a concept.
Demonstrate understanding of content by writing an essay.	Essay writing	Demonstrate understanding of content.

FIGURE 1.3: Separating the goal from the means.

Visit ***go.SolutionTree.com/differentiatedinstruction*** *for a free reproducible version of this figure.*

When we separate the goal from the means, we open many possibilities for students rather than limiting them to a particular pathway to reach the goal.

For example, consider one end-of-semester goal for my freshman students: "By the end of this course, students will be able to demonstrate their understanding of and reflection on the concept of neurodiversity." This goal does not have the means embedded within it. In practice, the students employ a wide range of means to achieve this goal. They might:

- Write journals and analyze how their thinking has changed over the course of the semester
- Conduct research into particular aspects of neurodiversity
- Interview neurodivergent individuals whom they know
- Write traditional essays
- Create works of visual art and present them
- Write songs and perform them
- Produce videos and show them
- Craft poetry or theater pieces and read them aloud

Regardless of the means, the overwhelming majority of the students meet the goal. As an educator, it is really exciting for me to see the variety of my students' journeys. I learn a great deal about my students, their thinking, and the concept of neurodiversity when they share their understandings and reflections.

By contrast, imagine that I stated my goal this way: "By the end of this course, students will be able to demonstrate their understanding of and reflection on the concept of neurodiversity by writing an eight-page paper and giving a formal presentation using a slideshow." This goal has the means embedded within it, and each of the various components of the means—in this case, writing the paper, giving the presentation, and using a slideshow—could act as a barrier for a student.

At the end of the day, lesson, activity, unit, or semester, what matters most is that our students work toward and achieve the goals we have set for them. How exactly they do that is far less important. After all, as educators, we care most deeply about our students' learning—we want them to gain new understandings, develop new skills, think more deeply and critically, and much more. We want them to get there. Mandating a particular pathway can result in a barrier that might prevent students from making the full journey and might make it impossible for them to reach the goal.

SPOTLIGHT: UNIVERSAL DESIGN FOR LEARNING

UDL is an educational framework for expanding learning opportunities for all individuals. Inspired by the concept of universal design in architecture, which strives to ensure the accessibility of physical spaces, educational researchers David H. Rose and Anne Meyer developed UDL in 1984 with the founding of CAST (Center for Applied Special Technology; www.cast.org). The mission of CAST is to "bust the barriers to learning that millions of people experience daily" (Open Access, n.d.). Since the mid-1980s, thanks to rigorous, ongoing research, CAST has developed the UDL Guidelines, resources, publications, and trainings that have reached numerous educators around the world (Rose & Meyer, 2006).

The three core principles of UDL are intended to inform the entire educational enterprise—planning, teaching and learning, and assessment (CAST, 2024). Specifically, when engaging UDL, educators should:

1. Design multiple means of engagement
2. Design multiple means of representation
3. Design multiple means of action and expression

At its heart, UDL facilitates expansion and flexibility in educational settings. CAST argues that, by engaging the UDL framework, educators can increase the likelihood of meaningful learning for every student through the design and implementation of a wider range of practices in planning, pedagogy, and assessment (Gordon, 2024).

STRATEGY 2: RECRUIT STUDENT INTEREST IN MORE THAN ONE WAY

As educators, we want our students to be involved and motivated. We wish for them to be interested in, excited about, and ready for learning. Unfortunately, though, as I discussed earlier in this chapter, sometimes the way that a teacher goes about getting students involved and motivated can act as a barrier for some students. To reduce or remove barriers to student engagement, educators should aim to recruit student interest in more than one way. CAST (Center for Applied Special Technology), in their guidelines for UDL, encourages teachers to "design multiple means of engagement" when they plan lessons and activities (CAST, 2024).

For example, a teacher might think a contest or competition would increase student interest and engagement, but it could end up creating a barrier for some learners. An elementary language arts teacher might create a series of scavenger hunt activities where students identify and correct grammatical errors, a middle school band director might hold an adjudicated solo performance festival, or a community arts teacher might engage judges for an art show. While these activities may help engage some students, they may act as barriers for individuals who become anxious in competitive environments, who hold themselves to perfectionistic standards, or who feel extremely uncomfortable when their work is publicly compared to that of their classmates.

Rather than utilizing only one approach to recruiting student interest, educators who recruit student interest in more than one way increase the accessibility of their teaching. Some other possible ways to recruit student interest include the following.

- **Sharing the work of the artist and the book that the teacher wishes to reference so that every student is familiar with them:** Essentially, the teacher provides the prior knowledge they wish to activate, lays out the context for what they are about to teach, and connects that context to the new material, concepts, or skills to ignite student interest and motivation. Letting all of the students in on the context that we wish to reference increases the accessibility of our teaching and helps boost student engagement and motivation.
- **Demonstrating what the students will be able to do as a way to spark the "wow" factor:** The teacher

can heighten student interest in and excitement about what they are about to learn through a high-quality demonstration. This demonstration could be executed by the teacher or through the use of recordings, visuals, or guest presentations. Showing students that they soon will know, experience, or be able to do something awesome—something that inspires a reaction of "Wow!"—drums up student engagement, helps motivate students, and increases the accessibility of what we are about to teach.

- **Providing choice:** Student ownership engages and motivates learners. Teachers can set parameters for students to make all sorts of decisions. For example, a band director could allow the students to select the final piece of repertoire for the upcoming concert by giving them three pieces to choose from, playing recordings of each one, and asking the class to vote on their favorite. A mathematics teacher could provide students with two possible homework assignments and ask them to complete one of them. Students in an English literature class could select one of four books to read and form a book club with the other students who chose the same text.

See the reproducible "Recruit Student Interest in More Than One Way" at the end of this chapter (page 51) for a tool educators can use to plan diverse ways to recruit student interest.

Recruiting student interest in more than one way increases accessibility by providing multiple entry points for students to engage with materials and activities, which makes embarking on the educational journey a real possibility for everyone.

STRATEGY 3: COMMUNICATE IN MORE THAN ONE WAY

As educators, we want to be sure our students understand information, instructions, and feedback. We want our students to take in, process, retain, and make meaning of what we communicate when we teach. Unfortunately, sometimes the way that teachers communicate can act as a barrier for some students, making it difficult for them to learn. To lessen this barrier, educators should aim to communicate in more than one way. The UDL Guidelines call for teachers to "design multiple means of representation" as part of their planning (CAST, 2024).

Providing students with instructions and information by telling them what you want them to know might feel as though it is an efficient pedagogical strategy, but it will not be sufficient for all students. For example, a student who processes auditory information slowly or a student who experiences challenges with interpreting and understanding language may not understand what you are saying. This creates a barrier that interferes with the student's learning and makes the educational experience less accessible.

Educators who communicate in more than one way increase the likelihood that students will understand them, thereby increasing the accessibility of their teaching. Some other possible ways to communicate include the following.

- **Employing visual tools:** Teachers can use visual tools as another way to communicate with their students. These may include words, pictures, symbols, discipline-specific notation, and more. Representing information visually can help more students gain access to the information and understand what is being communicated. I explore strategies for using visual tools, as well as the role of visual tools in accessible arts education pedagogy, in much greater depth in chapter 5 (page 143).
- **Defining terms:** Every subject area has its own vocabulary—its own language that is used to refer to elements and describe concepts or processes. Taking the time to define the terms they use can help educators communicate more effectively with their students. By doing so, teachers open more possibilities for student understanding, thus making the educational experience more accessible.
- **Utilizing technology:** Today's students choose to communicate using technology, whether it be through

texting, using apps for polling or educational games, taking and posting photographs, creating videos, or video conferencing. Educators who employ technology as a medium for communicating with their students make their teaching more accessible by using tools with which students are familiar and comfortable. The medium of technology might be just what a certain student needs to understand the teacher's message.

See the reproducible "Communicate in More Than One Way" at the end of this chapter (page 52) for a tool educators can use to plan diverse ways to communicate with students.

STRATEGY 4: ASSESS IN MORE THAN ONE WAY

Educators want to uncover meaningful evidence of student learning. We want to find ways for our students to show what they know and can do so their learning is seen and demonstrated. As I noted earlier, sometimes the assessments educators use cannot reveal all—or even some—of the learning that is taking place for a particular student. In these cases, the assessments become a barrier for the student because their learning is not visible through the window of the particular assessment. To lessen this barrier, educators should aim to assess in more than one way. When teachers "design multiple means of action and expression," using the parlance of the UDL Guidelines, they plan for a range of assessments, increasing the visibility of student learning (CAST, 2024).

To revisit one of the barriers I already discussed, assessing students based on how well they can execute a skill or on a public performance might feel like a terrific form of authentic assessment, particularly in skill-based or arts-based settings. After all, if we are teaching someone how to draw, how to play an instrument, how to dance, how to compute the average of a group of numbers, or how to diagram sentences (for just a few examples), it seems to follow that asking the student to do those things would be an effective way to assess their learning. However, merely assessing what a student can do is not a sufficient way to determine whether and how much a student has learned, even when that learning has to do with skill development. Sometimes, students have learned in other ways that they cannot yet demonstrate by executing skills or presenting a performance. For those students, the learning may be in their brains but not yet in their fingers, in their writing, or in their bodies. Employing one means of determining whether learning has taken place creates a barrier that interferes with student learning and diminishes the accessibility of the educational experience.

Teachers who assess in more than one way increase the likelihood that learning will be seen and demonstrated, thereby increasing the accessibility of their teaching. There are many possible ways to assess students. The following strategies offer a couple examples.

- **Looking beyond pencil and paper:** As we saw earlier in the case of the student and his ear-training tests, for some students, using pencil and paper can be a barrier to showing what they know and are able to do. They may have gained the knowledge and developed their skills but not be able to use pencil and paper to express what they know. Traditionally, many assessments include a pencil-and-paper component. Looking beyond pencil and paper requires educators to engage their creativity when it comes to assessing their students and to provide a range of opportunities and media by which students can show what they have learned. When the ear-training teacher took pencil and paper out of the assessment by utilizing manipulatives, she was able to see how much the student learned and was able to do when it came to ear training.
- **Exploring beyond *knowing equals doing*:** In the arts, as well as in many other subject areas, what a person knows is often bound up in what they can *do*. A person who can execute something well is generally considered to possess knowledge in that area. Educators often assess their students based on how well they perform a particular task, whether it be playing an instrument, dancing a choreography, solving mathematics problems, composing well-written essays, debating a topic convincingly, memorizing poetry,

> or reciting the spelling of words correctly, for just a few examples. However, *knowing* something takes multiple forms and has to do with more than execution. *Knowing* can also include the ability to understand concepts, explain something clearly, and detect and correct errors in the performances of others. Assessing in more than one way compels educators to seek, recognize, and validate multiple ways of *knowing* to more fully understand their students' learning.

When I was studying jazz voice performance, the level of my scat-singing performance was far below the level of my theoretical understanding. I had highly developed knowledge of music theory and the principles of jazz improvisation, but it was extremely difficult for me to translate that knowledge into successful scat singing. Thankfully, my teachers took full stock of what I knew about jazz improvisation and did not limit their assessments of my knowledge to how well I could scat-sing. It took many, many hours of practice, coupled with the guidance of my teachers, to get me to the point where I could perform vocal improvisations that reflected my understanding of the music.

Exploring beyond *knowing equals doing* requires educators to seek evidence for multiple dimensions of student learning, with the aim to ensure that learning is seen, demonstrated, and validated.

See the reproducible "Assess in More Than One Way" at the end of this chapter (page 53) for a tool educators can use to plan diverse ways to assess student work.

STRATEGY 5: UTILIZE TASK ANALYSES

Complex tasks can be a barrier for some students. The students might become overwhelmed by what is being asked of them. They might not know where to start—or, after they have begun, they might not have a clear understanding of how to proceed. An evidence-based strategy from special education known as a *task analysis* can be a very effective way to address this barrier (McConomy, Root, & Wade, 2022; Means, 1993).

A *task analysis* is a sequential list of the substeps of a complex task broken down into subtasks. As a result, (a) the task becomes more manageable because students can focus on and complete each individual, doable subtask, (b) the sequence of steps provides students with a process for completing the task, and (c) students have the opportunity to review and understand the entire sequence of steps at any point in the process.

The most effective task analyses break down the task into very small steps, with each step involving only one element. Multiple elements in a single step of a task analysis could be overwhelming for some students. Thinking about this another way, it is far more effective for a task analysis to contain more (rather than fewer) steps. Including too many steps in a task analysis does not present difficulties or barriers for students, but including too few steps could. When in doubt, add steps to the task analysis.

Task analyses are usually presented as lists. They can be represented in words, in words and symbols or pictures, or just in pictures, depending on the particular student, task, and setting. Consider the following sample task analysis for students to follow to clean up after they use watercolors in an art class.

1. Put your paintbrush into your water cup.
2. Use a paper towel to mop up any loose paint on your watercolor kit.
3. Close the cover of your watercolor kit.
4. Put your watercolor kit on the shelf where it is kept in the classroom.
5. Bring your paintbrush to the sink.
6. Turn on the cold water in the sink.
7. Clean your paintbrush by running it under cold water for thirty seconds.
8. Turn off the cold water in the sink.
9. Use a paper towel to blot extra water from your paintbrush.
10. Put your paintbrush into the canister where it is kept in the classroom.

11. Bring your water cup to the sink.
12. Pour the water in your water cup down the drain.
13. Run the cold water in the sink for thirty seconds.
14. Throw away your water cup.
15. Throw away your paper towels.
16. Bring your watercolor painting to the drying-station tables.
17. Leave your watercolor painting on an empty spot on one of the drying-station tables.
18. Return to your seat.

See the reproducible "Create a Task Analysis" at the end of this chapter (page 54) for a tool educators can use to create task analyses.

SPOTLIGHT: TASK ANALYSIS

Task analysis was first developed and articulated by special education researchers in the 1970s (Gold, 1976; Moyer & Dardig, 1978). In the years since, it has been embraced by special educators and behavioral therapists, who use it to promote individuals' skill development and to nurture their independence (Sam & Autism Focused Intervention Resources and Modules, 2016a). Task analyses can be effectively utilized in a wide range of contexts, beyond academic skills—from teaching daily living skills (hand washing, teeth brushing) to household skills (cleaning, cooking), to communication skills (active listening, providing appropriate responses; Pratt & Steward, 2020; SkyCare ABA, n.d.).

Teachers and students most often use task analyses in one of two ways (McConomy et al., 2022; Pratt & Steward, 2020).

1. **Forward chaining:** Starting with the very first step and ensuring that each step is mastered before moving on to the next step in the sequence
2. **Backward chaining:** Starting with the very last step and ensuring that each step is mastered before moving on to the previous step in the sequence

Task analyses can also be utilized as part of what is commonly referred to as *total task teaching*, where the student attempts the entire complex task while the teacher takes note of the subtasks in the task analysis that require additional support as a way to focus their instruction (Pratt & Steward, 2020; Sam & Autism Focused Intervention Resources and Modules, 2016a).

While most of the time, teachers create the task analyses that their students will use, it is possible for the development of a task analysis to be a pedagogical tool. I have created task analyses along with students—particularly students who have effectively used task analyses that were prepared by others. Together, we talk about and analyze the task, and the student takes the lead in determining the steps and their sequence. In some cases, after having codesigned several task analyses with me, the students began to write their own task analyses independently, without my assistance.

Takeaways

As educators, we can have a powerful impact on people's lives. It is one of the great rewards of our profession to facilitate students' growth and development. Helping learners make progress every day and hearing from former students that their time with you influenced them in positive ways are sources of deep satisfaction for every educator.

We can increase our impact by increasing access. When students have greater access to engagement, participation, and learning, educators can have an even more significant impact on students' lives. Accessible arts education provides frameworks, principles, habits of mind, and strategies that we can use to increase our impact on our students in at least two powerful ways.

1. **We can change students' educational lives.** By opening learning opportunities and experiences to everyone, we make it possible for all students to enjoy the marvelous human endeavors of expanding thinking, developing skills,

and coming up with new ideas, solutions, processes, creative works, and more. In other words, accessible arts education provides us with tools we can use to promote and facilitate meaningful educational opportunities for every learner.

2. **We can change students' feelings about themselves.** By providing multidimensional pedagogical approaches with a range of pathways to learning and various means of assessment, we create the conditions for all students to experience success and think of themselves as good students. Put another way, accessible arts education provides us with habits of mind and practices that can help us nurture student confidence.

I first engaged some of the principles, habits of mind, and pedagogical practices of accessible arts education by sheer instinct when I was teaching the remedial sections back in the mid-1990s. Today, accessible arts education is an established, dynamic, and generative framework that all educators can use to amplify their impact by increasing access.

In the Artist's Words

I'm very realistic about the arts industry. . . . I'm not disregarding how important my art is, but I know that sometimes I will be included in an exhibition or public programming because you've got to check that you've included a disabled artist. . . .
But you should know that if you do curate me into that exhibition, I'm gonna wedge open that door, and I'm gonna build a ramp and prioritize accessibility. And you know what? There will be so many disabled artists who will follow, and we will change the face of the art industry. It's not gonna stop with me. I'm your Trojan horse! (A. C. Mills, personal communication, September 25, 2024)

—**Amy Claire Mills**, textile artist, curator, and producer

Recruit Student Interest in More Than One Way

Use the following table to brainstorm a range of ways to recruit student interest. The table includes three specific ways to recruit student interest, as well as space for you to add other ways not listed here.

How I Plan to Recruit Student Interest	
Provide Background Knowledge or Experiences	
Demonstrate for the "Wow" Factor	
Provide Student Choice	
Other	

Accessible Arts Education © 2026 Solution Tree Press • SolutionTree.com
Visit **go.SolutionTree.com/differentiatedinstruction** to download this free reproducible.

Communicate in More Than One Way

Use the following table to brainstorm a range of ways to communicate with students. The table includes three specific ways to communicate, as well as space for you to add other ways not listed here.

How I Plan to Communicate	
Employ Visual Tools	
Define Terms	
Utilize Technology	
Other	

Accessible Arts Education © 2026 Solution Tree Press • SolutionTree.com
Visit **go.SolutionTree.com/differentiatedinstruction** to download this free reproducible.

Assess in More Than One Way

Use the following table to brainstorm a range of ways to assess student work. The table includes three specific approaches to assessment, as well as space for you to add others, as well.

How I Plan to Assess Student Work	
Look Beyond Pencil and Paper	
Explore Beyond Knowing Equals Doing	
Provide Student Choice	
Other	

Accessible Arts Education © 2026 Solution Tree Press • SolutionTree.com
Visit **go.SolutionTree.com/differentiatedinstruction** to download this free reproducible.

Create a Task Analysis

Use the following table to help you design a task analysis. Start by listing the complex task that you intend to teach in the left-most column. Next, create a list of sequential steps for completing the task. Then, break the steps from the preceding column into smaller steps. Finally, in the right-most column, break the smaller steps from the preceding column into even smaller steps.

Complex Task	List of Sequential Steps to Complete the Task	A Longer List of Sequential Steps to Complete the Task	A Still Longer List of Sequential Steps to Complete the Task

I think so many of us in the creative industries who are deaf, disabled, or neurodivergent realize you have to do some form of activism, some form of helping toward that social change to enable you and those behind you to have the career that you want to have. I think it's interesting because I think our generation, in a way, we've sort of missed the boat on some of these things because we're still paving. But those before us paved the way so we could be educated, those before them paved the way so that we didn't have to live in care homes. . . . Each generation of disabled people are paving the way for the next one toward equality, which, it's getting closer and closer. And I truly believe our industry is the way to create social change, but it's also been the one that creates the prejudice and the bias and all that other stuff because it currently tells our stories in very negative ways.

—Cherylee Houston,
disabled television and radio actress

CHAPTER 2

ENCOURAGE STUDENTS TO EXERCISE CONTROL AND AGENCY

It took me until graduate school to think deeply about the ways that power dynamics play out in education.

Let me pause for a moment to clarify what I mean here when I refer to power dynamics. I see *power dynamics* as the processes, relationships, structures, and interactions related to the ability to make things happen in a particular way. When the power dynamics are such that a person or a group of people has some power, they are able to direct or sway people, processes, or institutions toward a desired outcome. Power is intertwined with other concepts that I discuss in this chapter, such as control, agency, and influence.

Before I went to graduate school, I had thought a great deal about power in other contexts—political power, power in relationships, power in family systems—but I had not yet seriously considered education through the lens of power. It feels a bit embarrassing to admit this today (particularly in writing!), and it will likely surprise anyone who knows me and my work, particularly my students and colleagues. But the truth is that, when it came to issues of power in education, I was pretty naive before I got to graduate school.

That all changed when I encountered critical pedagogy as a first-year doctoral student. Reading works by influential educators like Paulo Freire (1970), Michael W. Apple (1979), Madeleine R. Grumet (1988), and so many others, such as Henry A. Giroux (1981), Peter McLaren (1989), and William F. Pinar (Pinar & Grumet, 1976), lifted the veil so I could finally see and understand the myriad ways power intertwines with teaching and learning. I began asking questions about the underlying power structures in education—questions like the following.

- "Who determines what gets to be taught?"
- "Whose knowledge and skills are considered legitimate, and why?"
- "How does the distribution of power in the educational process mirror other power structures in society?"

Having gained this newfound perspective on power and education, I couldn't unsee it. In fact, quite the opposite: For a while, power dynamics were the first—and sometimes the only—thing that I observed, everywhere I turned, as a student and as a teacher. And it was not a matter of passive observation. It provoked my emotions and compelled me to act.

On the emotional front, I found myself becoming increasingly frustrated and downright angry. I also felt a sense of doom because the underlying power structures in education appeared to be deeply entrenched, extremely problematic, and impervious to change.

I responded to these feelings by morphing them into action. Witnessing and contemplating these dynamics propelled me to disrupt them. While I was in graduate school, I seized opportunities to redistribute and equalize power, both as a student and in the teaching positions I held at the time. In letters, meetings, conversations, and demonstrations, I spoke up and acted out to find and create new ways that power could be shared among everyone who participates in the educational process—policymakers, administrators, teachers, students, and parents. These efforts were mixed overall. On some occasions, they were successful, primarily in small, baby-step ways, and on others, they were not, because there were simply too many immovable obstacles of one kind or another.

Based on the mixed results of these experiences, I turned my attention and energy to the arena where I could have the greatest impact: myself, as an educator and person, and the elements of my work that I can control and have the agency to change.

I made the commitment to myself—and to my current and future students and colleagues—that, throughout my career, I would do whatever I could to uncover and reconfigure power differentials in my own teaching, in the educational settings in which I work, and (potentially) in the field of education writ large, with the aim of making the educational process more just, fair, open, and equitable for everyone. This commitment has been a beacon throughout my career, and it continues to light the way for my work today.

This chapter illustrates how disabled people are often denied control and agency and how this impacts teachers' work with disabled students. You'll discover strategies for encouraging students to exercise the control and agency they do have in the short term while advocating for more just power dynamics over the long term.

Control and Agency

One way power plays out in education has to do with two related concepts: control and agency. Control and agency are expressions of power; they are both rooted in power, and power is intertwined with them. Put slightly differently, it is not possible for someone to have control or agency without also having at least some power.

Control is a form of influence. It involves the ability to make decisions and execute actions in ways that have an impact. The impact could be on people (including oneself), processes, structures, or things. It could be significant and obvious, or it could be small and barely noticeable. Another way of thinking about it is that control, by its very nature, requires an object (something that is controlled).

Agency is the ability of an individual or group to take action independently. It has to do with possessing the initiative and utilizing (or securing) the necessary resources to determine what action to take, set about the execution of that action, and actually carry out the action, all on one's own. The action could be grand and momentous, or it could be finely tuned and barely visible. What is important when it comes to agency is that the actors perform it independently.

In the Artist's Words

I've always enjoyed coming up with novel solutions, even before I got hurt. But when it comes to being disabled and coming up with system designs for doing certain things, it's really nice for me to come up with little fun plans for how to improve my daily life, and increase my productivity. Because with the drone photography, I have to find somebody, and then, you know, I have to go in my van, find spots. It can be challenging with my disability. So I have been thinking about a new project. You can get a microscope, and then I could do photography inside and then match the micro with the macro. That would be great. I could spin that in a really cool way for people to enjoy it. And I think it would be good for me. (M. Raynor, personal communication, September 23, 2024)

—**Matthew Raynor**, quadriplegic photographer

Consider for a moment where control and agency reside—and, more specifically, with whom they reside—in the educational enterprise. Let's begin by taking a look back before we turn to where things stand today.

For many generations, control and agency in educational settings resided primarily with teachers rather than students. Teachers were cast as the subjects who actively do the work of educating: planning the curriculum, facilitating lessons and activities, nurturing relationships with students, managing classroom behaviors, and assessing student work. Teachers were considered active agents in the educational process who exercise control over what takes place, how it unfolds, and what their students are expected to do. By contrast, students ended up being cast as the objects to whom education is done. Students were thought of as passive recipients of their education, which they could not control, rather than active agents in their education who have some control over what takes place and how they learn. In this traditional view, the students possess minimal (if any) control or agency in the educational process. Rather, the students merely do what their teachers ask and require of them.

Fortunately, the evolving thinking about education over many decades has made it possible for me to use the past tense when I write about this conception of education and its implications for control and agency. The evolution began when Freire (1970) excoriated the forces at work related to control and agency, as well as other manifestations of power differentials in education and society, in his groundbreaking book *Pedagogy of the Oppressed*. Freire's ideas led to an outpouring of publications, workshops, courses, and programs by scholars and practitioners who were eager to expose where control and agency lie, critique current structures of control and agency, reimagine those structures in the name of social justice, and bring people together to work to enact new, more just dynamics around control and agency in education and in society at large. Since that time, these efforts have continued and have grown tremendously—in size (that is, the sheer number of people participating), volume (that is, stronger, louder, and clearer), and complexity (that is, encompassing an increasing number of layers, streams, and elements).

As a result, most educators are aware of at least some of the ways that control and agency play out in their work with their students, reflect on what they can do to recognize and reconfigure those processes, and engage in thoughtful efforts to put their reflections into action in their classrooms and with their school communities. They are also much better equipped to see some of the ways that their students have exercised their control and agency, such as through acts of resistance or through self-expression. From my perspective, as someone who vividly remembers being part of educational interactions and systems that were bound to the traditional view of control and agency, it is deeply exciting and refreshing to witness this evolution. I no longer feel a sense of doom; on the contrary, I am optimistic about where the field stands today and where it is headed.

Yet we cannot rest on the laurels of how far we have come. There remains much to be done.

To start with, the forces of long-standing traditions in particular subject areas can act as a potent undertow to the flow of progress when it comes to control and agency in education. Considering table 2.1, there are many such instances in the arts.

TABLE 2.1: Control and Agency in the Arts

Possesses Control and Agency	Lacks Control and Agency
Theater director	Cast, crew
Musical ensemble conductor	Players, singers
Choreographer	Dancers
Exhibit curator	Artists
Client or patron	Hired artists

When it comes to subject areas outside of the arts, instances of the reign of tradition include those in table 2.2.

TABLE 2.2: Control and Agency in Non-Arts Subject Areas

Possesses Control and Agency	Lacks Control and Agency
Publisher	Creative writer, author
Editorial board	Scientist, academic researcher
Editor	Journalist
Funder	Researcher
Researcher	Research subject

Furthermore, an array of strong traditional forces has denied people with disabilities control and agency in virtually every aspect of their lives, including education. These forces continue to be pervasive in society today. Even as organizations and nondisabled people act with the best of intentions, the potency of the traditional forces remains extremely powerful. Due to the effects of these forces, far more often than not, disabled people possess limited control and agency (Brock, Schaefer, & Seaman, 2020; Mustaniemi-Laakso, Katsui, & Heikkilä, 2023).

Writings by notable disability self-advocates (Heumann, 2020; Kulkarni, Miller, Nusbaum, Pearson, & Brown, 2024; Ladau, 2021; West, McLaughlin, Shepherd, & Cokley, 2023; Wong, 2020) frequently highlight the following specific examples as representative of a much larger set of instances where disabled people are often denied control and agency. The full list of instances is quite extensive. Disability self-advocates and others in the field of disability justice have undertaken a great deal of theorizing about the dynamics behind that denial, though a more thorough discussion of the topic is beyond the scope of this book. At its extreme, the denial of control and agency plays out in the exclusion of disabled people because it is extremely difficult, if not impossible, to exercise control or agency in absentia.

- Disabled people often do not have the opportunity to participate in events, activities, initiatives, and the like. This may be due to barriers to accessibility (such as inaccessible physical spaces, lack of captioning or other accessibility supports, or websites with inaccessible fonts, typefaces, or formatting), or it may be because disabled people simply have not been invited. As a result, nondisabled people participate, and disabled people are absent.
- Disabled people often do not receive the important information or materials necessary for them to exercise control or agency in aspects of their lives and activities. This is usually due to barriers to accessibility, such as websites or documents that use inaccessible fonts or

typefaces or cannot be processed and read aloud by screen-reading technology or instances when announcements are made without amplification or American Sign Language interpretation. Under these conditions, disabled people are denied control and agency.

- Disabled people are often treated as less-than by nondisabled people or by organizations and institutions. For example, when a disabled person is assisted by an aide, a nondisabled person might speak with the disabled person by addressing the aide, not the disabled person themselves. Or perhaps a leader of an organization might use condescending and patronizing language when addressing disabled people. While not deliberate, these and other similar behaviors serve to infantilize disabled people, which denies them control and agency.
- The voices of disabled people are often missing from conversations, publications, and events about things that directly affect them. Instead, nondisabled people speak and write about and for disabled people. Speaking for oneself is one important way that people exercise some control over their lives, over how they are portrayed, and over how others view and understand them.
- Disabled people are much more likely to be unemployed than nondisabled people. According to the Bureau of Labor Statistics (2025), the unemployment rate in the United States for people with disabilities is two times that for people without disabilities. Disabled people are therefore two times more likely to be excluded from the workforce than nondisabled people. One meaningful way that people exercise some control is by securing gainful employment, which provides an arena where they can control aspects of their lives. Having a job also unlocks opportunities for people to activate agency in their lives by developing themselves as professionals and earning, saving, and spending their own money.

In the Artist's Words

I think that when we see a musician on stage, an orchestra, we don't see a lot of folks, at least on a visible level, with disabilities and I think that when we start at this age and we're thinking about ways that we're really shifting the training from a very early age of who can be in an orchestra, I'm hoping that not only are we providing a service that allows students to feel included and to feel happy and joyful through their music making, but we're also shifting where our fields can be. Especially in classical music, which has had profound accessibility issues on a variety of levels. (Bernard, 2022b)

—**Adrian Anantawan**, violinist and educator

Strategies to Encourage Students to Exercise Control and Agency

In educational settings, the project of attending to control and agency to nurture and expand fairness, justice, and equity is ongoing. While the profession has traversed a considerable—and very promising—distance in this regard over the last several decades, the traditional power structures and dynamics, though they may have been weakened, too often continue to hold. In the words of a common response to young travelers, "we aren't there yet." We therefore must continue our work to disrupt and extinguish traditional configurations of control and agency so we can eventually transfer more control and agency to our students. The strategies in the following sections provide some effective ways teachers can seek to encourage students to exercise control and agency in their learning settings.

Flattening the Hierarchy Between Teacher and Student

The hierarchical relationship between teacher and student can be a barrier to student control and agency. One way that educators can reduce that barrier is to create the conditions for flattening that hierarchy. For example, teachers can find opportunities to learn alongside their students, provide students with opportunities to share their unique knowledge and expertise, or seek ways to remove themselves from the center of the action in the classroom. Flattening the hierarchy between teacher and student might look like these examples.

- A middle school drama teacher asks students to critique his performance of a monologue and offer constructive feedback on what he could improve and how he can practice to make those improvements.
- A high school mathematics teacher asks a student to go to the whiteboard and demonstrate the steps the student used to solve a complex mathematics problem. The other students ask their peer questions about her process. Then they turn to a classmate and reflect together on what they learned.
- A dance teacher at a community arts program is not familiar with hip-hop dance. She engages a hip-hop-dance expert to teach several sessions of her class. During the sessions, the teacher participates as a student so that teacher and students are learning together.
- At the end of every class meeting, a high school science teacher hands out index cards with three questions on them: (1) What went well in class today?, (2) What could have gone better in today's class?, and (3) What questions do you have about today's class? Students provide their answers anonymously and hand the cards to their teacher as they leave the classroom. The teacher reads the cards and uses the student feedback to guide her as she plans for the next class session.

Figure 2.1 shows how the teachers in the previous examples might think about ways they can flatten the hierarchy between themselves and their students.

Activity	Control and Agency	Where Control and Agency Reside	Other Ideas
Student feedback on teacher monologue performance	a. Selection of monologue b. Performance c. Feedback	a. Teacher b. Teacher c. Students	Could the students select the monologue from a list?
Student demonstration of their process for solving a mathematics problem	a. Selection of student b. Demonstration c. Feedback d. Reflection	a. Teacher b. Student c. Students d. Students	Could a student volunteer to demonstrate a different approach to reaching the same answer?
Students learning hip-hop dance	a. Selection of guest teacher b. Participation in dance class	a. Teacher b. Teacher and students	Could the teacher ask a student to summarize the day's lesson with a short demonstration?
Student feedback on index cards	a. Selection of questions b. Responses to questions c. Use of feedback	a. Teacher b. Students c. Teacher	Could the students provide suggestions for questions they would like to see on the cards?

FIGURE 2.1: Flattening the hierarchy between teacher and student.

*Visit **go.SolutionTree.com/differentiatedinstruction** for a free reproducible version of this figure.*

When the hierarchy between teacher and student is lessened, teachers can share aspects of control and agency in the classroom with their students. Sharing comes up in relation to the next strategy that we will consider: teachers sharing their decision-making processes with their students.

Sharing Decision-Making Processes With Students

Another way teachers can address the power differential between themselves and their students is to share their decision-making processes. As they learn about their teachers' decision-making processes, students gain a greater understanding of various aspects of their education and begin to see themselves as partners alongside their teachers. In the spirit of that partnership, students have the opportunity to respond to, offer feedback on, and comment on the decision-making processes their teachers share and the decisions their teachers have made. As they become more informed, students develop a sense of control over aspects of their education.

Teachers make a multitude of decisions every day as part of their work, most notably content decisions (about what they are teaching), pedagogical decisions (about how that teaching is taking place), and management decisions (about how to handle situations as they arise). While the outcomes of these decisions affect the students, students often do not know much, if anything, about the teacher's reasoning behind their decisions or about their decision-making process. When teachers let students in on the thinking that led to their decisions, they provide students with an opportunity to exercise control in their education.

One easy and effective way for teachers to share their decision-making process is in the realm of content—specifically, talking with students about what they are teaching and why. Explaining what students are learning and why they are learning it helps them understand the broader context and objectives that drive curricular decisions. Consider the following examples of what this might look like.

- A visual arts teacher explains to her tenth-grade class that they are working on a watercolor project in today's session because it is an introduction to a unit on water and its role in visual art. Throughout the unit, they will explore various ways that visual artists have used water in their work, as well as art pieces about water or that portray water.
- A second-grade teacher tells her students they are learning about money and how to make change in this week's classes as a first step to an interdisciplinary unit where they will create and operate a class store. The activities in the unit will combine mathematics, social studies, visual art, and language arts. At the end of the unit, they will invite the school community to purchase items at their store.
- A private piano teacher explains to her adult student that she is practicing the fingerings for all major scales to develop the dexterity and strength necessary to execute those same fingerings when she plays musical pieces.

Making the processes and reasoning behind their decisions more transparent is an important way that teachers can encourage student control and agency. A key way that teachers can operationalize student control and agency is through the use of carefully curated and supported opportunities for student choice.

Providing Opportunities for Student Choice

Sometimes, it is possible for students to make choices as part of their education. They might be able to make choices about content (what they will work on), process (how they will go about an activity or project), peers (with whom they will collaborate), or assessment (how they will demonstrate their learning and growth), for just a few examples. When students have the opportunity to make decisions that affect them, they can exercise their agency.

To be clear, these choices are not intended to be wide-ranging or open-ended—on the contrary, they require well-defined structures and parameters to be effective. When students have the freedom to choose, within specific constraints, educators can provide opportunities for student choice while still ensuring that their learning goals and objectives are being met. Providing opportunities for student choice might involve the following options.

- **Content**
    - A middle school language arts teacher asks her students to choose one of three novels to read for their next project. She provides the class with synopses of the books, and each student makes a selection.
    - A community chorus director invites the choir to choose the next piece of repertoire they will learn. He plays recordings of three pieces, and the choir members vote for the piece they like best. The ensemble will learn the piece that receives the most votes.
- **Process**
    - A high school dance teacher assigns a choreography project to groups of four students. At the end of the project, the student groups must perform an original dance sequence they have created. The students can go about the process of creating and preparing their choreography as they wish, as long as they have a final presentation ready by the due date.
    - Students in a community visual arts class have just returned from a visit to the local art museum. The teacher asks them to respond to the artwork they viewed and share their responses with the class. They can choose to respond by writing a reflection in a journal, creating a piece of art using materials in the classroom, or researching the artwork and writing an essay about what they learned.
- **Peers**
    - In their general music class, elementary-aged students are working on playing an arrangement of a song using xylophones. The teacher has asked the students to

spend class time practicing their parts. They can practice alone, in pairs, or in small groups. The students are allowed to choose whether they will collaborate as they practice and with whom.

+ Middle school drama students are working on scene study. Their teacher asks the students to select a classmate who will be their scene partner. Together, the pairs of students will practice their scenes, memorize them, and perform them for the class.

- **Assessment**
  + Young students in a third-grade mathematics class have just completed a unit on multiplication. Their teacher has prepared several stations around the room with different multiplication activities. Students must complete the tasks at two stations for their unit assessment. The first station has worksheets with pencil-and-paper multiplication problems. At the second station, students video-record themselves responding to multiplication flash cards. The third station features a computer game where students try to complete as many multiplication problems as they can in two minutes. At the fourth station, students use blocks to illustrate what it looks like to multiply numbers.
  + College students in a first-semester writing course have the option of completing their final paper in any of the following genres: personal narrative, essay, short story, play, or poem. Their professor has provided overarching guidelines for the assignment as well as specific requirements for each genre so that students understand what is expected of them for their final assignment.

Figure 2.2 (page 72) shows how the teachers in the previous examples might think about ways they can provide opportunities for student choice.

Opportunities for Student Choice				
Activity	**Content**	**Process**	**Peers**	**Assessment**
Reading assignment	Choice of novel			
Rehearsal for concert	Choice of repertoire			
Choreography project		Creation of choreography		
Museum visit		Responses to artwork at the museum		
Preparation of xylophone piece			Practice of the xylophone piece	
Preparation of scenes			Scene study	
End-of-unit multiplication				Multiplication stations
Final writing assignment				Paper genre

FIGURE 2.2: Providing opportunities for student choice.

*Visit **go.SolutionTree.com/differentiatedinstruction** for a free reproducible version of this figure.*

The benefits of encouraging students to exercise control and agency are many and varied, for teachers and students alike (Banger, 2022; Furlonger, Garner, Callaghan, Foreman, & Bryson, 2020; Jacobs, 2023). Using the strategies I described in this section, teachers can create the conditions for their students to become active partners in—rather than passive recipients of—their education. No longer merely the objects of the educational process, students can gain the agency and control to be the subjects—or, at least, the cosubjects—of their learning journeys.

Furthermore, when teachers encourage students to exercise control and agency, students can reap benefits beyond the walls of a particular classroom. For example, speaking on behalf of a classmate who is having trouble getting to school because of a lack of transportation, a student might request assistance for them. Or a group of students might meet with their principal to discuss a school policy they feel is unfair. Or a student with hearing loss might self-advocate by requesting that microphones be used by those who speak at schoolwide events. As teachers encourage their students to exercise control and agency, they begin to create welcoming spaces in the school community—spaces where students can provide feedback or raise issues, with the knowledge that their teachers will listen to their concerns, take them seriously, and try to find ways to help.

Takeaways

As educators, we all wish for our students to learn, grow, thrive, and succeed. There are few things in life more rewarding than the tremendous pride we feel when we see our students come into their own and shine or when we run into a former student and hear all about their triumphs. At the same time, our students' success is inextricably linked with our planned obsolescence as their teachers. It is often said that a teacher has been successful when their students no longer need them—when they have become obsolete.

Issues around my own planned obsolescence recently moved to the foreground. I wrote this book during the very first sabbatical of my career. (My previous institutions did not offer sabbatical leave.) Being on sabbatical meant stepping away from my day-to-day duties as the leader and director of academic programs and an institute that I both created and founded. The graduate music-education programs and the Berklee Institute for Accessible Arts Education are deeply interwoven with my identity and are extremely close to my heart. It was not easy to leave them behind, even for just a semester.

While it is human nature to desire to feel uniquely valuable and needed—and I certainly wish to feel that way—during my sabbatical, it was essential for me to trust other people to teach courses, advise students, administer programs, collaborate in meetings, handle situations, make decisions, and execute tasks (among many other things). Furthermore, I needed to remind myself that the real success of the sabbatical (aside from completing this book!) would be for those whom I had trusted to handle the various facets of my job in my absence to have done so smoothly, effectively, and successfully. The control and agency they exercised would be signs of my effectiveness as an educator and administrator.

Gone are the days when all the control and agency in the educational process resided with the teacher—when every aspect of teaching and learning was teacher determined, teacher implemented, and teacher focused. Teachers bring a sensitive awareness of issues of control and agency to their work with their students, and they actively seek pathways to encourage their students to exercise control and agency. The strategies I discussed in this chapter offer a few avenues for you to explore as you support student control and agency in your teaching.

When we encourage our students to exercise control and agency, we lay the groundwork for their independence as learners and as human beings. We set the stage for them to no longer need our guidance, support, or instruction. The role that we as educators can play in helping our students exercise control and agency within and beyond our settings—whether they be studios, classrooms, rehearsal halls, community centers, or elsewhere—is one of the true privileges of our profession.

In the Artist's Words

For a long time, I didn't know how to express myself. I felt like I had to explain my disabilities, but explaining doesn't resonate with people. It doesn't connect with others when you're not being emotional about it. . . . You can say you have cerebral palsy, but [people] don't really know what that means. So now I use my disability and art blog and express things like, this is what it feels like to go down the stairs with cerebral palsy. Here's what it's like to have your mind going a mile a minute with ADHD. Here's what it feels like to have PMDD [premenstrual dysphoric disorder]: Imagine yourself driving a car. You feel in complete control. You feel confident that if something happens, you can navigate your way out of it. You've done it before, and you'll do it again. That is, until you're taken hostage, shoved in the trunk, and the kidnapper starts driving a hundred miles an hour with no regard for anything or anyone around you. . . . Your emotions become completely out of control and it feels like there's no way to grasp the steering wheel. That's a scary feeling. And so, I try to use all these forms of art to evoke emotion out of people rather than to explain what it is, because people tend to connect more with the emotional piece of it. (B. Raucci, personal communication, September 20, 2024)

—**Briana Raucci**, photographer, visual artist, and designer

I left school when I was fourteen and had a really bad few years with anxiety and panic attacks, and just—I wasn't diagnosed autistic then, and we just didn't really know how to deal with it. It all just got too much. But when I was in school, I used to go up to the music rooms at break and lunch because I didn't want to be around anyone. I would take myself up to the music room and I would just play piano and I would sing. I'd never had any training. I think I had one piano lesson at primary, and I just bashed away and sort of learned how to play piano and would sing, and it was a really good outlet for me.

—Ella Bouvard,
musician and para-athlete

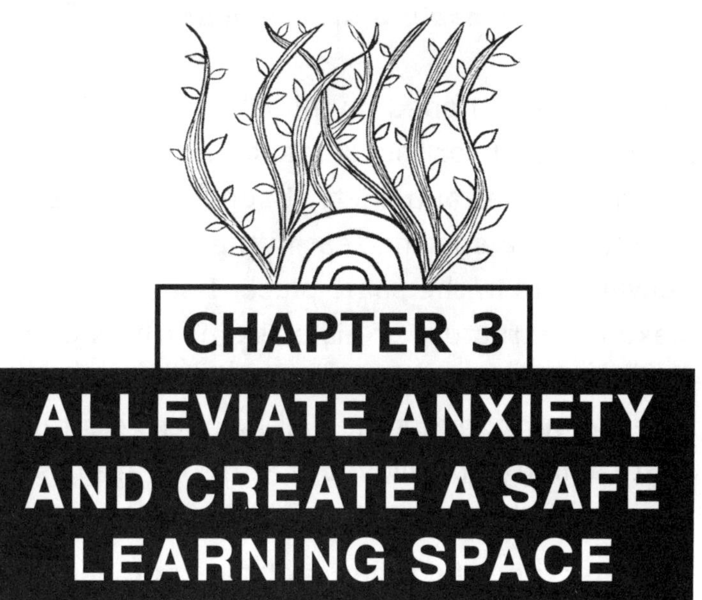

CHAPTER 3
ALLEVIATE ANXIETY AND CREATE A SAFE LEARNING SPACE

Recently, one of my colleagues stopped me in the hallway with questions about how to handle a situation in one of his college music theory classes. He told me there was a student in the class who spent every session sitting in the back of the room, refusing to join her peers or participate. He said, "This student is noncompliant. I don't see how she'll be able to succeed in the class."

Not having met the student or observed the class, I asked my colleague some questions: "How often does the class meet? Does the class meet in the same room every time? Do the students have assigned seats? How are class meetings structured?" Behind these questions was my search for barriers that might be preventing the student from participating in the class. My hunch was that the student might be experiencing anxiety, that this anxiety was a barrier to her engagement, and that her response to the anxiety was to sit in the back of the room, removed from her classmates and from the teacher.

My colleague explained that the class meets three times per week, always in the same room. The students sit wherever they would like; their seats are not assigned. When I asked him about the structure of the class meetings, he said, "Oh, the class is different every time. We just take things as they go."

His responses strengthened my hunch that anxiety might be a barrier to engagement for this student. In the interest of reducing or removing the barrier of anxiety, I suggested that my colleague assign each student a specific seat in the classroom so that everyone always sits in the same place. I spoke with him about ways to make the structure of his class meetings more consistent as well as ways to share that structure with the students. He seemed pleased to leave our conversation with concrete strategies he could bring to his teaching and relieved that the strategies would not require him to alter his curriculum or his pedagogy.

Two weeks later, he called me to let me know that the student whom he had thought was noncompliant was now sitting alongside her peers, participating in class activities, doing her homework, and demonstrating improvement. He said, "I don't know how you did that—you worked a miracle! You didn't even need to observe the class or know anything about the student. Thank you!"

So, how was I able to figure out what was behind this behavior without having met the student and without having observed his classes? I brought a different mindset to the situation. His interpretation that the student was noncompliant is an easy one to make: The student is not complying with the requests of the instructor or with the requirements of the course. But the mindset of accessible arts education does not stop with the easy interpretation; rather, it requires educators to think beyond the student's behavior and ask, "What else could be going on?" A student's lack of engagement and participation in class in and of itself is not necessarily evidence of noncompliance—it is only evidence of nonengagement and nonparticipation. There is a key difference here: If the student was saying something that was noncompliant (such as, "No, I won't do that!") or was taking an attitude of noncompliance through their body language or facial expressions, then we might be able to make a stronger argument that the student truly was noncompliant. That wasn't the case in this situation. All we had to go on was the student's lack of engagement and participation. By engaging the frameworks and habits of mind of accessible arts education, I was able to search for possible barriers to this student's participation and suggest some ways to reduce or remove them.

This chapter explores some ways teachers can strive to alleviate student anxiety and create safe learning spaces in arts education settings at all levels. To set the stage for the strategies, the chapter begins with a discussion of student anxiety and its implications for students with disabilities. The text provides strategies for reducing and removing anxiety as a barrier to student learning.

Student Anxiety

Numerous studies of student anxiety have been conducted over the last several decades. While the investigators may explore different questions, or the studies may have different areas of focus, there is widespread agreement in the research community that a large—and growing—number of students of all ages experience anxiety when they are in school and other educational settings. An extensive review of research in 2023 related to academic stress and anxiety suggests that student anxiety is pervasive to the point that it has "become normalized in students' lives" (Jiménez-Mijangos, Rodríguez-Arce, Martínez-Méndez, & Reyes-Lagos, 2023, p. 3638). In the report *Anxiety in Children*, Zhen Wang and colleagues (2017) state that one in eight children is affected by childhood anxiety disorders. The Centers for Disease Control and Prevention (CDC, 2025) reports that the percentage of students aged six to seventeen who have been diagnosed with anxiety increased from 5.5 percent in 2007 to 6.4 percent in 2011–2012, and the percentage of students aged three to seventeen who have been diagnosed with anxiety was at 9.4 percent in 2016–2019. In her article for *NEA Today*, a publication of the National Education Association, Mary Ellen Flannery (2019) describes student anxiety as an epidemic that starts with children as young as four and five years old and continues through college and graduate school. The Cleveland Clinic (n.d.a) reports that 15 to 20 percent of children and adolescents are affected by anxiety disorders.

When students feel anxious, they are not able to learn effectively. For decades, studies have shown that student anxiety can be a significant barrier to student engagement, student learning, and academic achievement. A 1978 publication about the relationship between anxiety and academic achievement states that "anxiety interferes with the academic achievement of college students" (Rosenfeld, 1978, p. 151). More recently, psychologists Maisha M. Syeda and Jac J. W. Andrews (2015) note that the anxiety that young people experience "interferes with their school functioning" (p. 29). Researcher David Mathew (2015, 2016), who has studied student anxiety extensively, argues that learning is a fragile enterprise, and this is due in large part to the barriers to student learning, engagement, and achievement that student anxiety creates.

Student anxiety may present itself in a variety of ways. Some manifestations of student anxiety have to do with what the student will *not* do rather than something the student does. For example, a student experiencing anxiety:

- Might not volunteer to speak in class
- Might not participate in activities
- Might not be willing to try something new, fearing that they will make a mistake or fail
- Might not attend class
- Might not ask for help
- Might try to avoid tasks, activities, or situations that provoke their anxiety

Other manifestations of student anxiety can be seen in things that the student does. For example, a student experiencing anxiety might:

- Apologize every time they make even the slightest error
- Try to change the subject to avoid a task, activity, or situation that provokes their anxiety
- Act out in class to avoid doing something that makes them anxious
- Tremble or start to cry when they are feeling anxious

While these various forms of expression differ from one another, they stem from a singular underlying issue: anxiety. Student anxiety can be a significant barrier to engagement and learning. For students to learn effectively, educators must understand student anxiety and work to alleviate it. Furthermore, when it comes to students with disabilities, the prevalence of anxiety is greater than it is in the general population.

Student Anxiety and Students With Disabilities

While many students experience anxiety, students with disabilities are often navigating additional sources of anxiety related to their disabilities and diagnoses. Researchers have reported a greater prevalence of anxiety in children with disabilities compared to their nondisabled peers. As one example, a meta-analysis of numerous studies revealed that children and adolescents with intellectual disabilities experience elevated rates of anxiety more frequently than children without disabilities (Brunelle, Abdulle, & Gorey, 2020). Other researchers have learned that college students with disabilities report greater anxiety and stress compared to their nondisabled peers (Coduti, Hayes, Locke, & Youn, 2016; Ford, Wenner, & Murphy, 2019; Hendrickson, Woods-Groves, Rodgers, & Datchuk, 2017). Greater rates of anxiety have also been reported in research on adults with disabilities compared to adults without disabilities. According to a study by the CDC analyzing adults across the United States, those with disabilities report experiencing frequent mental distress 4.6 times as often as adults without disabilities, with the prevalence for the former at 32.9 percent and for the latter at 7.2 percent (Cree, Okoro, Zack, & Carbone, 2018).

The additional anxiety experienced by people with disabilities often comes into play in educational settings. Consider the following brief examples of how it might look.

- Many students with disabilities may feel anxious about whether they will be singled out because of their disability. Will their peers treat them differently or think about them differently because of the accommodations or supports they will need to use?

- A student who uses a wheelchair may feel anxious about the pragmatic elements of moving through various spaces and participating in class activities. Are all spaces and activities accessible for students who use wheelchairs?
- A student who needs additional time to process spoken or written language may feel anxious about whether they may require more time than their classmates to respond to the teacher's questions, instructions, or prompts. Will they feel as though they look less intelligent or less capable to their peers or to the teacher?
- A student with autism may feel anxious about whether they fully understand what will be expected of them in a learning session. Will they know what they are expected to do, what they are expected to say, and how they are expected to behave in various situations?
- A student with hearing loss may feel anxious about whether they will have access to all materials and experiences in the class. Will they miss out on critical learning and participation opportunities because of their hearing loss?

The previous list provides just a few examples. There are many, many ways that students with disabilities might experience additional anxiety in educational settings.

Strategies to Reduce and Remove the Barrier of Student Anxiety

When arts educators engage strategies designed to reduce and remove anxiety as a barrier to learning, they pave the way for "miracles" like the one I described earlier in the chapter. It can seem miraculous when you witness what can be possible when a student feels safe in a learning environment.

Here's how you might explore new possibilities when you encounter student barriers.

- Develop a hunch about a possible barrier that might be at play when it comes to this student's participation in class. Create a hypothesis about the student's experience. (In the experience I shared, I wondered whether the student might be experiencing anxiety that was preventing her from feeling sufficiently safe to participate in class. This became my hypothesis about what else might be going on in this situation: Perhaps the student was feeling anxious.)
- Test your hypothesis by asking questions to uncover whether the particular situation might include that barrier. (The questions I asked about the structure of the classes and the use of the physical space in the classroom revealed opportunities to reduce or remove anxiety as a barrier to student engagement, participation, and learning.)
- Identify a couple of simple strategies to try. (I framed my suggestions to my colleague in ways that would make it more likely that he would implement them, offering a few small changes he could make to his teaching right away without requiring him to overhaul his curriculum or his pedagogy.)

In this case, my hunch was correct, and the barrier turned out to be student anxiety, which can be reduced or removed by using various strategies that make the classroom a safe space for the vulnerability that comes with learning.

The following sections contain some of the most potent teaching strategies when it comes to lessening student anxiety and creating an environment where students feel safe and can be vulnerable as they learn.

Creating and Communicating Structure in Class Meetings

Knowing what is happening and being informed about what is about to happen are important forms of agency for all of us. While there are some people who may enjoy giving themselves over to the unknown and unexpected, generally speaking, most of us like to know what is going on and what is going to happen next.

This knowledge gives us a sense of agency, safety, and control. Rather than being passive, uninformed beings, we generally like to feel that we are active and informed.

When it comes to educational settings, researchers confirm that students would rather engage with their teachers and be active, knowledgeable agents in the educational enterprise than be uninformed about the process and have their education be "done to" them (Brame, n.d.; Hyun, Ediger, & Lee, 2017). Students prefer feeling active and informed when it comes to their learning, and helping students feel active and informed can contribute to the reduction or removal of student anxiety as a barrier to learning.

One way teachers can share information about what is going on and what is going to happen next in their classrooms, studios, and ensemble rehearsal halls is by creating, communicating, and following a consistent structure in each session. Doing so can provide students with agency, safety, and control. It can also help make our teaching spaces feel safe for learning by addressing student anxiety.

All educational experiences, whether they are classes, individual lessons, or rehearsals, feature two simultaneous structures as they unfold: (1) the macro structure and (2) the micro structure. Let's take a closer look at each.

THE MACRO STRUCTURE

The *macro structure* has to do with the overall flow of a class meeting. It is the big-picture structure of the kind of events that unfold and the order in which they typically happen. When I speak with educators about the macro structure, I ask them about what usually takes place at the beginning, middle, and end of their time with students.

An example of a macro structure for a middle school visual arts class might look something like this.

- **Beginning**
  a. Students enter the room and go to their assigned seats at tables.
  b. Directions for a short "do now" activity are on the board. The materials that students will need for that activity are laid out on their tables.
  c. Students complete the "do now" activity.
- **Middle**
  a. The teacher brings the students together and leads a discussion about the activity.
  b. The teacher makes a connection between the "do now" activity and the day's lesson.
  c. The teacher gives a short minilecture or explanation of the day's lesson and introduces a project or activity.
  d. Students work on the project or activity on their own, with the teacher going around to check in with each student, answer questions, and provide feedback.
- **End**
  a. The teacher brings the students together for a wrap-up reflection and discussion.
  b. Students put away their materials and store their projects.
  c. Students leave for their next class.

An example of a macro structure for a high school mathematics class might look something like this.

- **Beginning**
  a. Students enter the room and go to their assigned seats.
  b. The teacher brings the students together and reviews the homework assignment.
- **Middle**
  a. The teacher makes a connection between the homework assignment and the day's lesson.

b. The teacher gives a short minilecture or explanation of the day's lesson and introduces a project or activity.
c. Students work on the project or activity on their own, with the teacher going around to check in with each student, answer questions, and provide feedback.

- **End**
  a. The teacher brings the students together for a wrap-up reflection and discussion.
  b. The teacher hands out and explains the homework assignment.
  c. The teacher hands out index cards.
  d. Students write one thing that they learned today and one question that they have on the index cards.
  e. Students hand in their index cards as they leave for their next class.

The reproducible "Planning the Macro Structure" at the end of this chapter (page 111) offers a tool educators can use to plan the macro structure of their classes and lessons.

Consistency is the hallmark of the macro structure. Class sessions will tend to unfold along the lines of the macro structure most of the time. Most days, the beginning, middle, and end of the meetings will look and feel the same in terms of the sorts of activities that take place, the roles of the teacher and the students, how people are positioned in physical space, and the overall flow of the way the meeting occurs.

There will certainly be occasions when class sessions don't follow the macro structure, such as just before an exhibition of student artwork, or when the students are starting a new unit, or when a guest artist visits the classroom, for just a few examples. However, more often than not, the macro structure holds true. Its consistency is what makes it an effective structure.

Furthermore, the macro structure's consistency is what makes it a valuable tool for reducing or removing the barrier of student anxiety. A consistent macro structure makes it possible for students to gain a strong sense of what to expect when they come to our teaching spaces, leading to positive outcomes. For instance, with a consistent macro structure, students can:

- Develop a stronger sense of safety
- Come to understand that they have some control over what happens when they are learning
- Become more comfortable in the space—with their classmates, with the teacher, and with the learning activities
- Grow in their ability to engage, participate, take risks, and learn

Finally, the macro structure can be more effective if it is done and not spoken. In other words, it is not necessary for teachers to communicate the macro structure explicitly to their students, for a couple of reasons. First, the macro structure refers more to a session's overall flow than to its specific components. Its effects come from a more subliminal sense by students that they know, overall, how the meetings will go when they come to your teaching space. Second, the macro structure is implicit within the micro structure, and teachers should definitely communicate the micro structure explicitly.

THE MICRO STRUCTURE

The *micro structure* has to do with the order of events that will take place in a single class session. It is the "agenda" of exactly what the teacher and students will do together, listed out in chronological order.

Most educators are accustomed to thinking about the micro structure because it is closely tied to their lesson plans. School-based educators are often accustomed to thinking about the micro structure because, in many cases, they are required to write the micro structure for every class meeting on the board as part of their compliance with state and local educational regulations.

An example of a micro structure for a private voice lesson might look something like this.

1. Physical warm-ups
2. Breathing warm-ups
3. Vocalization warm-ups
4. Repertoire piece 1
5. Repertoire piece 2
6. Repertoire piece 3
7. Discussion of homework to practice for next lesson

An example of a micro structure for a fourth-grade social studies class might look something like this.

1. Opening announcements
2. Last night's homework
3. Group reading and research activity on the civil rights movement
4. Group sharing of what they learned
5. Wrap-up and closing announcements
6. Homework for next time

The reproducible "Planning the Micro Structure" at the end of this chapter (page 112) offers a tool educators can use to plan the micro structure of their classes and lessons.

While simply providing the micro structure for students can be helpful for educators, actually using the micro structure makes it a more effective tool for reducing or removing the barrier of student anxiety. I like to refer to using the micro structure as *telegraphing the agenda*.

When teachers telegraph the agenda, they speak explicitly about the micro structure and help students see exactly how it relates to what is happening in the class. They let students in on their thinking about the order of class activities, as well as any decisions that they might need to make in the moment regarding necessary changes to the micro structure during the class.

Telegraphing the agenda for the private voice lesson previously mentioned might look something like this.

"This is what we're going to do today. . . ."

At the beginning of the lesson, the teacher shows the micro structure to the student and reads it through with them.

"Let's get started with our physical warm-ups. . . ."

The teacher names the first item of the micro structure using the same words that are written on the board so it is super clear to the students exactly what the teacher is talking about. If possible, the teacher points to the item on the board.

"We just finished our physical warm-ups. Next, let's move on to our breathing warm-ups. . . ."

The teacher walks the student through the micro structure, explicitly stating what they have just done and what they are about to do. If possible, the teacher points to the items on the board.

This process continues for all items in the micro structure until the lesson is over.

Telegraphing the agenda for the fourth-grade social studies class previously mentioned might look something like this.

"This is what we're going to do today. . . ."

At the beginning of the lesson, the teacher shows the micro structure to the students and reads it through with them.

"Let's get started by looking at last night's homework. . . ."

The teacher names the first item of the micro structure using the same words that are written on the board so it is super clear to the students exactly what the teacher is talking about. If possible, the teacher points to the item on the board.

> "We just finished talking about last night's homework. Next, let's move on to the group reading and research activity on the civil rights movement. . . ."

The teacher walks the students through the micro structure, explicitly stating what they have just done and what they are about to do. If possible, the teacher points to the items on the board.

This process continues for all items in the micro structure until the class is over.

Sometimes, teachers need to deviate from the micro structure once the lesson or class is underway. Some reasons for this could be outside the teacher's control, such as unanticipated interruptions, fire drills, and other nonpedagogical elements that affect the class session. There are also some reasons to deviate from the micro structure that are within the teacher's control. These might be pedagogical considerations the teacher makes in the moment, such as when a student or group needs more time to work on a particular item or activity than anticipated or when the teacher sees that changing the sequence of the elements of the micro structure would help facilitate student learning.

Whatever the reason, teachers should communicate about the deviation from the micro structure and the reasons for it as soon as they realize they will make a deviation. By explicitly explaining that there is going to be a change in the micro structure, telling the students what that change will be, and providing the reasoning behind the change, teachers help maintain students' feelings of safety and control in the classroom.

Communicating about a deviation from the micro structure of the private voice lesson might sound something like this.

> "Now that I have seen how you've been working on this aspect of your vocal technique, I think it would be better to switch the order of piece 2 and piece 3 in today's lesson and go to piece 3 first."

Communicating about a deviation from the micro structure of the fourth-grade social studies class might sound something like this.

> "Looking at today's agenda, since the fire drill took up some of our class time, we might not be able to finish the group reading and research activity. We'll check in toward the end of class, and if we need more time to finish, I'll make sure we set aside time in our next class."

Put another way, these moments when we deviate from the micro structure present a unique opportunity to engage students as partners in their learning. That partnership—and the agency it provides for our students—goes a long way as we strive to reduce and remove the barrier of student anxiety.

Preparing Students for New Experiences, Materials, and Activities

Learning is a vulnerable enterprise that requires students to take risks. Educational settings, by their very nature, often cast students in a deficit position. This could be the position of being the one who does not know certain concepts or how to execute certain skills, or it could be the position of being the one who has not engaged in certain experiences. After all, students are taking part in their education to learn new concepts, master new skills, and engage in new experiences—all in pursuit of their growth and development as individuals, artists, and members of society. However, it is important to remember that, for students, being positioned as one who does not know or who has not experienced something can provoke anxiety.

Two related strategies can help teachers reduce or remove student anxiety related to new experiences, materials, and activities: (1) preparatory narratives and (2) previewing. The following sections look more closely at each.

PREPARATORY NARRATIVES

A friend and I recently went to our high school reunion together. We have known each other for many years, and we have a great deal in common, but we are also quite different in one key aspect: I am an extrovert, and she is an introvert.

I could hardly wait to catch up with people from my high school class whom I hadn't seen in several years. My friend clearly felt differently. She was extremely nervous and anxious as we were driving to the venue. I tried to make conversation about something other than the reunion, hoping to take her mind off what was making her feel anxious. My friend had something else in mind.

She started asking questions, such as:

- "Who do you think is going to be there?"
- "Will there be name tags?"
- "Will the event start with a cocktail hour?"
- "Will there be a sit-down meal?"
- "What will people be doing?"
- "Will there be music and dancing?"
- "Will there be an after-party?"

As I responded to her questions, I realized that my friend was preparing for the experience by constructing a story that could help alleviate her anxiety about attending the reunion. She was striving to understand what would be expected of her and to think through the order of events so she could visualize herself at the reunion. My friend was using our conversation to craft what I like to refer to as a *preparatory narrative*.

Preparatory narratives can be useful tools to help reduce and remove anxiety in a number of situations. This proved to be true for my friend. As we drove home after the reunion, she told me our conversation helped her feel less anxious about the event and enjoy reconnecting with our classmates.

The most effective preparatory narratives in educational settings share particular features and are used in particular ways.

Specifically, they are first-person preparatory narratives that can help an individual get ready for a new situation or learn a new routine. They allow the person to imagine engaging in the new experience or routine, step-by-step, as a means of visualizing their participation and success. They lessen the newness and uncertainty by making a novel experience more concrete and by clarifying the individual's role. They can also assist with managing negative emotions that may come up by normalizing them and demonstrating that the person is not alone in their feelings.

The most effective preparatory narratives for educators share the following five key features.

1. **They are in the first person, most often the first-person singular.** These narratives are told from the perspective of the person who will engage in a new experience or learn a new routine. This makes the narrative more immediate and meaningful for the individual who reads it. The reader is the narrative's main character. For example, "Today I am having my first dance performance" could be the opening sentence to a preparatory narrative written in the first-person singular.

   Most often, these narratives are written for individuals rather than for groups, but there are occasions for which a preparatory narrative might be written for a group of students—for example, to help the whole class learn the routine for going to an assembly at school. In those cases, the narrative will be written in the first-person plural. An example of this might be, "Today we are going to the auditorium for an all-school assembly."

2. **They walk through the various events of the new situation or routine in chronological order.** These narratives provide the reader with the opportunity to envision themselves engaging in the new situation or routine, step-by-step, in order, from beginning to end. They prepare the reader for an unknown experience by making it more concrete, which lessens the person's anxiety. Understanding how the experience will unfold, step-by-step, can increase

the reader's sense of control and confidence, as they will know what to expect and can feel secure in their knowledge of the experience. For example, a preparatory narrative about a dance recital might be, "First, I will go to the warm-up room to do my stretches. Then I will go to the greenroom to wait until the stage manager tells me that it is my turn to perform. I can watch the other performers on the television screen in the greenroom while I wait. When the stage manager calls my name, I will go on stage and perform my routine. At the end of the routine, I will take a bow while the audience applauds. Then I will return to the greenroom to wait until the recital is over. I can watch the other performers on the television screen in the greenroom while I wait. When the recital is over, I will go to the lobby to see my family and friends."

3. **They validate and normalize negative emotions that might come up in the new situation or routine.** New experiences can often bring about negative emotions. Preparatory narratives validate and normalize negative emotions by helping the reader understand that their negative emotional response is not unique. Understanding that the negative emotions they might experience are the same emotions other people might experience makes the reader feel less alone. This helps reduce the reader's anxiety about how they might feel in the new situation. A statement that normalizes negative emotions in a preparatory narrative about a dance recital might be, "I'm nervous about my dance recital. This is OK. Lots of dancers are nervous at their first recital."
4. **They conclude positively.** These narratives always end happily. The endings of preparatory narratives focus on how the person thinks and feels about the new experience or routine afterward and share the individual's positive frame of mind and positive emotions. These conclusions have nothing to do with what happened during the experience

or routine; rather, the narratives end by stating positive thoughts and feelings about the experience or routine. An ending for the preparatory narrative about a dance recital might be, "I'll be happy and proud of myself when I'm finished." This text focuses on the positive emotions that the person will experience at the end of the dance recital. It says nothing about how well the individual performed at the recital. It does not describe how the audience responded to the person's performance. It does not mention what the dance teacher or anyone else had to say about how the performance went. What actually took place in the performance is not relevant to the narrative. It is about how the individual feels and what the individual thinks about the experience.

5. **They communicate the same overarching storyline.** While the specifics of preparatory narratives vary based on the experience or routine they describe, they all share a common overarching storyline, which can be summarized with the following text.
   a. "I am going to engage in a new situation or routine."
   b. "Here is what will happen and what I will do, in chronological order, step-by-step."
   c. "I may feel some negative emotions. That is OK. Everyone feels negative emotions in this situation or routine."
   d. "I will feel good and will think positive thoughts when the experience or routine is over."

The message of this storyline is that engaging in a new situation or routine can be—and will be—a positive experience. The content of the specific narrative helps make the details of the new situation or routine concrete and comprehensible. Together, the storyline and the content of preparatory narratives can help reduce or remove the barrier of student anxiety about the new situation or routine.

Figure 3.1 shows how an educator might plan preparatory narratives.

Reader: Sixth-grade students **New situation or routine:** Field trip to science museum	
"I am going to engage in a new situation or routine."	• Every year, the sixth graders in my school take a field trip to the science museum. This is my first time going to the science museum.
"Here is what will happen and what I will do, in chronological order, step-by-step."	• I will bring home the permission slip for the field trip so my parents can sign it, and I will bring the signed permission slip to my science teacher. • On the day of the field trip, I will line up with my classmates. • I will walk with my classmates to the bus that will be waiting for us outside the school. • I will sit quietly on the bus. I will listen to the chaperones and will follow their instructions. • When the bus arrives at the science museum, I will follow the chaperones' instructions and will get off the bus with my classmates. • I will stay with my classmates when we enter the museum. • I will stay with my classmates as we walk around the museum and look at the exhibits. I will follow the instructions of the chaperones. • When it is time to leave the museum, I will walk with my classmates to the school bus. I will get on the bus and will follow the chaperones' instructions. • When the bus arrives back at our school, I will wait for the chaperones to tell me to get off the bus. Then I will get off the bus and walk with my classmates into the school building and back to our classroom.

"I may feel some negative emotions. That is OK. Everyone feels negative emotions in this situation or routine."	• I am nervous about going to the science museum because it is a new place. That is OK. Many people feel nervous when they are going to new places. The chaperones will be there to help me, and I will be with my friends and my science teacher.
"I will feel good and will think positive thoughts when the experience or routine is over."	• I will be glad that I had the opportunity to go to the science museum with my classmates.

FIGURE 3.1: Preparatory-narrative planner.

Visit ***go.SolutionTree.com/differentiatedinstruction*** *for a free reproducible version of this figure.*

Preparatory narratives can take many forms. They can be written, hard-copy documents with words, pictures, symbols, and various combinations of these. They can be digital documents. They can be video or audio recordings. The form that they take should be customized for the student in order to make the narrative as accessible, meaningful, and useful as possible.

Preparatory narratives for students in preschool through second grade, for multilingual learners, and for students who have difficulties processing text tend to include more pictures or symbols than words. I have worked with kindergarten teachers who created narratives that consisted of mostly blank pages with a sentence at the bottom of each page. Students would fill the remainder of each page by drawing their own pictures in reference to the sentence on the page.

One of my former students who teaches music in a local urban school district created a preparatory narrative video to help his students prepare to give their concert in another school building across town. He recorded the video from the student's perspective, step-by-step, including boarding, riding, and exiting the bus to get to the building; entering the building; walking to the greenroom;

walking onto the stage; and walking off the stage. As the students watched the video, they were able to see exactly what they were going to see when they went to the new building and performed in their concert.

For students in middle and high school and for adults, preparatory narratives tend to consist mostly of text. I have created narratives to help college students develop a routine for effective studying. Depending on the preferences of the individual students, these narratives have been in the form of either paragraphs of text or bulleted lists. Using the narratives to guide them, the students were able to develop routines that improved their study habits.

High schoolers, college students, and adults can create their own preparatory narratives. I once sat next to someone on an airplane who used an audio recording of a narrative that she wrote about the safety of air travel and how to deal with unexpected turbulence. People can also compose narratives for others. When one of my colleagues shared with her graduate students that she was feeling anxious about her upcoming dental surgery, her students developed a preparatory narrative for her.

Creating effective preparatory narratives is an important first step. Using the narratives in multiple ways is critical for them to be effective tools to help reduce or remove the barrier of student anxiety in arts education settings.

Using a preparatory narrative can look something like the following.

- The teacher and the student(s) read or watch the entire narrative together.
- The teacher and the student(s) discuss the narrative. They may choose to read or watch excerpts as part of the discussion.
- The teacher provides a copy of the narrative for the student(s). This may be a hard copy of images, text, or both; a digital copy of images, text, or both; or a digital copy of audio or video files.

- If the teacher provides the narrative in hard-copy format, it is advised that the pages be laminated to preserve them well.
- The student(s) read or watch the narrative on their own as many times as they wish to do so.
- The teacher and the student(s) read or watch the entire narrative together at additional meetings if it continues to be relevant.

Unlike some other tools and strategies in accessible arts education, students typically use preparatory narratives many times. Teachers are often surprised to learn how many times students of all ages wish to read or view them. When I ask students about this, they tell me that engaging with a narrative makes them feel good, and because it makes them feel good, they want to read or view it again and again. It is as though each time a student reads or views the narrative, they are reassured once again about the new situation or routine, and their anxiety lessens. This is an important reminder for educators that, for many of our students, anxiety is an ongoing issue that requires our ongoing support. This stands in stark contrast to other barriers to student engagement and learning that teachers can reduce or remove by applying a particular strategy that can fully address an issue as it occurs, such as by providing materials with larger text sizes for students who need them.

While they are commonly used by special educators, other educators, generally speaking, do not know about preparatory narratives and therefore do not use them with their students. When I facilitate workshops and consultations about accessible arts education with educators in arts and non-arts subjects, participating teachers very often mention preparatory narratives as one of the key takeaways from our time together. Some educators have even combined curricular activities with the creation and use of these narratives. For example, there are music educators who have written narratives in the form of songs, language arts educators who have engaged students in writing poems that are preparatory narratives, and dance educators who have developed movement-based narratives set to music. However one creates and uses them, preparatory narratives can be a very effective strategy for reducing and removing the barrier of student anxiety in arts education settings by helping prepare students for a new situation or routine.

SPOTLIGHT: PREPARATORY NARRATIVES

I developed the term *preparatory narratives* to refer to stories of various kinds, and in various media, that any individual can use in advance of any new experience or routine. The most effective preparatory narratives:

1. Lessen anxiety about the unknown experience or routine
2. Make the unknown more concrete with specific information and a play-by-play sequence
3. Normalize negative emotions that might arise
4. Illustrate that the new situation is a bounded period of time, with a beginning, middle, and end

Social Stories™ are a subset of preparatory narratives—they are stories designed to assist autistic students with social situations (Carol Gray Social Stories, n.d.). In 1990, while she was teaching students with autism in the Jenison, Michigan, public schools, educational consultant Carol Gray developed, dubbed, and trademarked Social Stories (Carol Gray Social Stories, n.d.). A few years later, she collaborated with colleagues on a compilation (Gray et al., 1994) and a research article about their use (Gray & Garand, 1993). Gray's research, development, and publication efforts have continued over the decades, and she offers workshops and trainings, as well (Carol Gray Social Stories, n.d.). Research by others on the use of Social Stories and their effectiveness has been inconclusive, due in large part to the studies' very small sample sizes (Como, Goodfellow, Hudak, & Cermak, 2024; Leaf et al., 2020).

For more than thirty years, special educators, therapists, and parents have used Social Stories as Gray defined them and as she intended. These individuals have also created and utilized what I call preparatory narratives: stories with a wider population (people with other disabilities and diagnoses and individuals who do not have a disability or diagnosis) and for a greater range of purposes (for any new situation). Because Gray's definition and trademarking of Social Stories are not well known among practitioners, the preparatory narratives are often misnamed as Social Stories (ABA Educational Resources, n.d.; Autism Little Learners, n.d.).

PREVIEWING

Students might become anxious when they encounter new materials or engage in new activities for the first time in the presence of others. This anxiety stems from students not wishing to be vulnerable or to show any weakness in front of other people, whether that be the teacher or their peers.

Previewing can be an antidote to this aspect of student anxiety by helping students prepare for new materials and activities. When teachers preview materials and activities, they provide them for the students in advance of the class meeting in which students will use them (Edunators, n.d.).

Previewing serves two important purposes for teachers. First, it helps students prepare for the next session by making it possible for them to engage with the new materials and activities on their own and feel more ready to learn when they come to the next class meeting. Second, it helps make the bridges between class meetings more explicit for students, engaging them as partners in their learning who understand the ways that today's class and the next class are connected. This aids students in making sense and meaning of their learning in a more cohesive and coherent way (Positive Action, 2025). Consider the following examples.

- **Previewing new materials for a community-arts-school dance class:** At the end of the class, the teacher shows a video of the choreography that the students will be working on in their next session. She provides the students with a link to that video so that they can watch it again on their own. By giving students the opportunity to experience and gain access to new material before the teacher presents it in class, the teacher lessens the students' anxiety about working on something unfamiliar in front of their peers and the teacher.
- **Previewing new materials for a high school language arts class:** At the end of the class, the teacher introduces students to the book they will read for their next unit and explains that they will discuss the book's author and its historical and cultural context at their next class meeting. The teacher provides the students with links to information about these aspects of the book for them to review on their own. By giving students the opportunity to learn about topics that will be discussed in their next session, the teacher lessens the students' anxiety about discussing something new in front of their peers and the teacher.
- **Previewing new activities for a middle school chorus rehearsal:** The choral director announces that, next month, the students will begin working on a new music reading curriculum with new activities and materials, including music theory worksheets, sight reading exercises, and music dictation quizzes. Each rehearsal this month includes one of the new activities so that students have the opportunity to gain experience with them before they become part of their regular work in chorus. By working through these activities together in class before they are required of them, the students become familiar with the activities, are ready to learn with them, and are less anxious about engaging in something new.

Because digital audio recordings, video recordings, websites, and documents are readily available, simple to make, and easy to transmit, educators can preview new materials and activities without much additional work or effort. Previewing, while not a heavy lift for teachers, can help make student engagement and learning more effective by lessening student anxiety and helping students understand some of the ways that each learning session relates to the next.

SPOTLIGHT: PREVIEWING

Accessible arts education often expands the concepts and applications of more narrowly defined educational approaches because these approaches, when more broadly conceived and implemented, promote accessibility. Previewing is one example of this sort of expansion.

I use the term *previewing* to describe strategies educators can use to provide information, materials, and activities for students before they will be used in a class meeting. Effective previewing can help alleviate student anxiety and promote student learning. Previewing has broad applicability: Educators can utilize it in all subject areas, in all teaching and learning settings, and with all students.

By contrast, the published works of scholars and practitioners conceive of previewing more narrowly and with more limited usage. Specifically, they define previewing as a set of procedures for students with autism, ADHD, dyslexia, and learning disabilities to interact with texts before they read them, with the aim of improving their reading comprehension (Bansal, 2014; Capin & Vaughn, 2017; Melani, Mulyadi, & Firdaus, 2024; Ukrainetz, 2016). These include reviewing the headings and structure of the text, making predictions about the content of the text, identifying and examining important words and pictures, and locating and looking up unfamiliar terms (IRIS Center, n.d.; Lexia, 2023; Positive Action, 2025; Richards, n.d.).

Attending to Physical Aspects of the Classroom Space

Every educational space is a unique world. It is set up in a certain way, with its people, furniture, materials, lighting, and sounds in specified places and configurations. The world of an educational space also has its own culture, with common (often unspoken) practices and understandings that have to do with how people interact within the space, who gets to control which aspects of the space, and what sorts of behaviors are considered acceptable by whom in the space.

The larger context for the teaching setting plays a significant role in the ways that educators can control, change, and customize their educational spaces. Educators who have their own classrooms all day can control, change, and customize many more aspects of their teaching spaces than those who travel from room to room, either on a cart or in a university setting, or those who share spaces with many others in community arts organizations.

Within that larger context, teachers can strive to reduce or remove student anxiety as a barrier to learning by creating and maintaining consistency in the physical aspects of the classroom space to the degree that they can. One such aspect is the configuration of furniture and other large items in the space. Another is the use of assigned seats for students. Taken together, consistency in these two aspects of the physical space can play a significant role in lessening student anxiety and increasing students' sense of control and agency in the classroom. These strategies also clarify what is expected of students at the outset of a class session, setting them up for success.

When the configuration of the classroom is consistent, students can enter the space confident that they will be able to move effectively through the room because they can predict where people, furniture, and other items will be located. While this consistency helps make the classroom space more accessible for every student, it can be especially helpful for students with physical or motor challenges (Cheon, Reeve, & Vansteenkiste, 2020; Early Learning Ventures, n.d.; Rohrer & Samson, 2014).

When seats are assigned, every student knows they are required to be situated in a specific place in the room. They know where they are expected to be and how the space will look and feel to them from the perspective of their assigned seat. Strategies that attend to the consistency of the classroom space help students feel that the physical space is predictable, calm, and safe (Butay, 2023; Kidd, n.d.; Luther, 2023). Assigned seating is a common feature in many educational settings, particularly those that are based in elementary, middle, and high schools. Collegiate and community settings are less likely to require assigned seating.

Let's look at an example of using assigned seating in a theater class in a community arts organization. The theater teacher has established a routine with her students: The students enter the room and take their assigned seats at the beginning of every class session, before any activities will take place. Even though many of the activities in the theater class will require students to move around the room and leave those assigned spots, starting every class meeting with all students in their assigned seats establishes a routine that helps all students feel safe and lessens their anxiety. When students arrive, they know where they are expected to go and what they are expected to do right away. The routine helps the students feel empowered and in control as members of the class, and they can begin each class session with confidence.

If, for some reason, a teacher wishes to make any changes to the configuration of the classroom or the student seating assignments, they should provide their students with advance notice. Preparing students for these sorts of changes will help alert the students that the classroom space will be different from the way it has been. It will also help students understand in advance exactly how the classroom space will be different.

Let's imagine what it might look like to prepare students for changes to the configuration of an elementary music classroom. The elementary music teacher tells his students that they will be starting a new unit next week. In this unit, the students will be working together on several large-group activities and pieces that will require all students to be able to see each other as they play instruments and clap rhythms. The teacher explains that he will be changing the students' seating arrangement for the new unit. Beginning next week, the students will sit in assigned seats in a circle formation rather than in the rows that are the current classroom configuration. Providing the students with notice of the change in how they will be arranged in class can help alleviate anxiety by preparing them for what would otherwise be a sudden and unexpected change.

These strategies can help ensure that students are not surprised in the moment by these alterations to their classroom space. In-the-moment surprises can be a source of student anxiety and discomfort, which then can become a significant barrier to student learning. Preparing students rather than surprising them in the moment is one key way to reduce or remove that barrier and make the educational experience more accessible.

Emphasizing Consistency, Predictability, and Clarity of Expectations

The strategies to alleviate student anxiety and create a safe learning space that I described in this chapter share three common features: (1) consistency, (2) predictability, and (3) clarity of expectations. Students can become anxious when spaces feel chaotic, when there is a great deal of unanticipated change, and when they do not know what is expected of them. Fostering consistency—for example, in the structure of class sessions and in the layout and use of the space—can help lessen any sense of chaos, drama, or disarray for students. Seeing to it that students can predict what will take place by telegraphing the agenda and by preparing students for any alteration to their classroom space or class routines can serve to diminish the amount of unanticipated change students encounter. Making expectations clear through preparatory narratives and previews of new materials and activities can ensure that students understand what is expected of them.

As is the case for all accessible arts education strategies, every student can benefit from the approaches I discussed in this chapter, regardless of whether the student has a disability or diagnosis (Bernard, 2023). The strategies of accessible arts education are necessary for some students and helpful for all students. Starting with accessibility from the very beginning as we set up our teaching spaces and plan our lessons and units helps ensure that every student can engage in making art, participate in arts experiences, and learn and grow as an artist in a meaningful way.

Takeaways

Learning is a vulnerable act. When we learn, we make mistakes. We show how little we know or understand. We try things that we have never done before, and there is the real possibility of failure. We make tentative moves, and we sketch out newly formed thoughts and ideas.

The vulnerability inherent in learning can generate anxiety in our students. That anxiety can then act as a barrier to student engagement, participation, and learning. Alleviating student anxiety and creating a safe learning space are critical ways to make educational experiences of all kinds more accessible for all students. The strategies in this chapter address ways educators can increase consistency, predictability, and clarity of expectations in their teaching, all of which can contribute to creating an environment where students feel safe and can engage in the vulnerable—and remarkable—act of learning.

In the Artist's Words

Two nights ago, all of a sudden, I just got really anxious, like—it was so heavy—and I was like, "Oh my gosh! I just can't breathe right now. I'm so anxious!" And I have a staff person that kind of hangs out with me where I live, and I was like—I told her I'm anxious, I don't know what to do, and then I said, "Let's write a song! And we'll call it 'Anxious'!" And I just started playing these chords on the piano that coincided with that feeling, and I was like—I just started singing, "I'm anxious. I'm tight, and I'm confused," and these words just started coming out, and that's pretty much my process for any song. (Bernard, 2024a)

—**Jennifer Msumba**, autistic musician, author, and filmmaker

Planning the Macro Structure

Use the following table to plan the big-picture structure of your class meetings by outlining what will usually take place at the beginning, middle, and end of the class or lesson.

Big-Picture Structure for a Class or Lesson	
Beginning	List the elements in order, as many or few as applicable.
Middle	List the elements in order, as many or few as applicable.
End	List the elements in order, as many or few as applicable.

Accessible Arts Education © 2026 Solution Tree Press • SolutionTree.com
Visit **go.SolutionTree.com/differentiatedinstruction** to download this free reproducible.

Planning the Micro Structure

Use the following table to plan the micro structure of your class meetings by listing each item of the agenda in chronological order.

Agenda to Share and Telegraph
List the items in order, as many or few as applicable.

Accessible Arts Education © 2026 Solution Tree Press • SolutionTree.com
Visit **go.SolutionTree.com/differentiatedinstruction** to download this free reproducible.

I'm actually very dyslexic, so everything I have to learn I have to put onto audiotape. You know, so I can listen to it like I'm listening to you now . . . in my headphones. And I have a number of friends that will help me, or my partner will help me and read it backward, and forward, backward, and forward and such.

—Mark Beer, theater, film, television, and radio actor

CHAPTER 4

USE MULTIPLE MODALITIES AND PEDAGOGICAL APPROACHES

I'll never forget the time I was giving a professional development workshop to a group of about eight hundred piano teachers from a large region of the United States on how to make private piano lessons more accessible. We were at the strategies portion of the session—the part of the afternoon where I boiled down the frameworks and principles we had already discussed into specific ways that the attendees could change their teaching practice to make it more accessible.

I spoke about the fact that there have been long-standing traditions in arts education, specifically in how piano lessons are taught. As an example, I observed that I spent my entire education as a piano student sitting at the piano, with my piano teacher sitting in a chair next to the piano. I joked that I don't think my piano teacher ever saw me standing up, and I had no idea how tall or short my piano teacher was because we were glued to those seats, in those positions, every single time we met. We were glued to the tradition along with the seats.

I encouraged the piano teachers in attendance to step away from this tradition. "Think of all the other ways students can learn the piano," I said. "Ask them to clap; get them to move around the room. Have them stand up, gesture, sing, and speak the music. When your students step away from the bench, new learning opportunities and pathways become possible, and your lessons become more accessible for every student, no matter how they learn best." Essentially, I was urging the piano teachers to think more broadly about the modality of their teaching and about their pedagogical approaches to private piano lessons.

I was stunned by their responses. Hands shot up around the room. Some teachers shook their heads. Others wrote furiously in their notebooks. And some people started conversations with their neighbors. The atmosphere in the room took on a decidedly negative, tense tone.

I had clearly struck a chord (pun intended). When I called on someone who had raised her hand, she said, "What you're describing isn't going to work. If we did those things, we wouldn't be teaching piano lessons anymore. In piano lessons, the student sits at the piano, and they play."

I was flabbergasted. I didn't think my suggestions had been all that radical, nor had they come out of nowhere. They built on and flowed from the foundations and frameworks that we had been working with that day. But clearly the teachers felt otherwise. This group of piano teachers wasn't ready to step away from tradition. I was disappointed and sad to discover that, by holding so tightly to only one, traditional way of teaching piano, these music educators and their students would miss out on many opportunities for student learning and creative teaching. At the same time, there was only so much I could do in a single three-hour professional development workshop, and our time together was coming to a close.

So, I pivoted. Continuing as planned was not going to work. Instead, I engaged the tools and mindset of accessible arts education to make the remainder of the workshop accessible to the people in the room. From the perspective of accessible arts education, the teachers' adherence to the traditional piano lesson format was a barrier to their learning in our session because it prevented them from adopting teaching strategies that deviated from that tradition. I focused on meeting the attendees where they were: in a traditional piano lesson context. I went on to share and demonstrate the remaining teaching strategies with the understanding that they would be part of piano lessons where the student sits at the piano and plays.

This approach is one of the key practices of accessible arts education: recognizing a barrier and responding to that barrier in real time by adjusting one's teaching to better reach the participants. Being responsive to barriers that emerge as our teaching unfolds is a critical aspect of effective accessible arts education. Accessible arts education involves both planning and improvising. In addition to anticipating barriers to engagement (as I discussed in chapter 3, page 84), educators respond effectively to barriers that make themselves known as they are teaching and as students are learning, doing, and working.

If the educators had been able to discuss alternative ways of learning piano, what might that have looked like? In addition to the traditional approaches to learning the piano, for just a few examples, a student might:

- Sing the passage they are working on as a way to demonstrate the phrasing, articulation, and dynamics they hope to achieve when they play the passage on the piano
- Walk around the room using their gait and body movements to illustrate aspects of the music, such as the contour of the melody, the ebb and flow of the phrasing, the articulation of the notes, and much more
- Write a story to go along with a piece they are learning as a way to imbue the music with characters, a plot, and an overall arc
- Compose a piece in the style of a composer they are studying
- Write their own lyrics to a piece they are playing
- Create an alternate ending for a piece they are playing
- Improvise in the style of a piece they are learning

Because people learn in a wide variety of ways, engaging multiple modalities of teaching and learning makes it possible for more students to access educational experiences. Or, put in the opposite way, teaching in only one way—through engaging a singular modality—can act as a barrier to those students who learn best through a modality that the teacher did not engage.

This chapter shares some ways teachers can widen the range of teaching modalities and pedagogical approaches they employ in their teaching. I explore the idea of multiple learning modalities, expanding our understanding beyond the widely accepted notion of "the big three" (visual, auditory, and kinesthetic). Finally, I end the chapter by considering what it looks like to engage a wide range of pedagogical approaches.

Learning Modalities

Many educators I meet seem to have the same understanding of *learning modalities*, or the ways that people learn. That shared understanding can be summarized as follows.

- People learn in different ways.
- The three primary ways that people learn are (1) visual, (2) auditory, and (3) kinesthetic. These ways of learning are referred to as *learning modalities*.
- Most people learn best through one preferred learning modality. Teachers think about their own preferred learning modalities as a way of relating to their students. They might refer to themselves, for example, as a "visual learner," an "auditory learner," or a "kinesthetic learner," and they might use those terms to describe their students, as well.
- Teaching is more effective when a learner is engaged through their preferred learning modality.

I am continuously reminded in my conversations with educators that the preceding points are universally accepted as fact. Research studies confirm my experience. According to a 2014 investigation, over 90 percent of teachers believe in the concept of visual, auditory, and kinesthetic learning modalities (Howard-Jones, 2014), and an analysis of the texts used in introductory courses in education and educational psychology finds that 80 percent of these texts discuss the concept of visual, auditory, and kinesthetic learners (Wininger, Redifer, Norman, & Ryle, 2019).

However, the history of the use of the concept of learning modalities, and particularly the notion of preferred learning modalities, tells another, more complicated story. Educational scholar Thomas Fallace (2023) chronicled and analyzed the history of the visual, auditory, and kinesthetic learning modalities, which are often referred to in the literature as *learning styles*, and he arrived at some fascinating conclusions.

- The concept that students prefer a particular learning modality—either visual, auditory, or kinesthetic—dates back to the early 1920s.
- This idea was initially utilized in relation to individuals with learning disabilities, particularly those with reading challenges, with the aim of determining and then utilizing a student's preferred learning modality to better facilitate their reading skill development.
- The practice of determining a person's learning modality preference expanded in the 1960s to include non-White students in urban settings, with the aim of addressing inequities in education.
- By the 1970s, educators of all learners were applying the concept of preferred learning modalities.
- The application of the idea of a preferred learning modality was never intended to expand beyond the context of remedial reading.
- The notion that students have a preferred learning modality and therefore learn more effectively through that modality has never been supported by empirical research.

In summary, Fallace's (2023) conclusions confirm what other researchers have argued for decades: The very popular and generally accepted (among educators) notions that there are three learning modalities, that all people prefer one learning modality, and that engaging someone's preferred learning modality will result in more effective teaching lack evidence to support them (Cassidy, 2004; Fallace, 2023; Kampwirth & Bates, 1980; Kirschner, 2017; Pashler, McDaniel, Rohrer, & Bjork, 2009; Stahl, 1999; Willingham, Hughes, & Dobolyi, 2015).

Multiple Learning Modalities

A different way of thinking about and utilizing learning modalities has taken root in education since the 1980s. Rather than conceiving of learning modalities as a typology with which to classify students and then tailoring one's teaching to a student's preferred learning modality, educators have come to consider their teaching through the lens of multiple learning modalities. Grounded in and supported by the extensive and highly influential scholarship of Howard Gardner's (1983) theory of multiple intelligences and CAST's UDL Guidelines (CAST, 2024; Orkwis & McLane, 1998), this perspective encourages educators to both vary and expand the number of the teaching modalities they employ as a way to ensure more students can learn, and it argues that the learning that does take place when multiple modalities are engaged is more meaningful for students. Educators' shared understanding of multiple learning modalities can be summarized as follows.

- Effective teachers should engage multiple learning modalities when they teach, for two main reasons.
    a. By activating multiple learning modalities, educators can reach students no matter which learning modality is best for them.
    b. By being engaged in multiple learning modalities, students can learn more effectively because their learning will be more deeply and meaningfully embedded in their understanding. Put another way, learning "sticks" better if it takes place through more than one learning modality.

This way of thinking about and engaging multiple learning modalities resonates with the principles and practices of accessible arts education by celebrating learner variability and by underscoring the educator's responsibility to expand the range of ways in which they teach to facilitate the wide variety of ways students learn.

In the Artist's Words

My music education background continues to be instrumental in my writing. It helps with pacing, theme, characterization . . . everything. And while I do musical theater for fun, music theory informs so much of *everything* that I do creatively. . . . There's so much with rhythm, or when I'm acting, pitch and inflection too. So it applies to single lines of dialogue. But then there is also story structure and theme—where you introduce a theme, then build on it, then return to that theme with a variation that changes its meaning and emotional resonance. There's setups and payoffs and key changes—crescendos and decrescendos, harmony and dissonance, it all builds to a climax and resolution. And a lot of it I've ingrained subconsciously, which I think is where you want to get to? (Bernard, 2024b)

—**Jeremy Andrew Davis**, writer, film director, disability advocate, and representation consultant

Multiple Learning Modalities and Arts Education

One reason the concept of multiple learning modalities rings true for arts educators is that the arts, by their very nature, are multimodal endeavors. Artistic engagement—whether that be creating, performing, improvising, or responding (or any combination of these)—involves visual, auditory, and kinesthetic engagement.

At the same time, however, it can be said that there is a dominant modality to some art forms, specifically dance, music, and visual arts.

- Dance and the kinesthetic modality
- Music and the auditory modality
- Visual arts and the visual modality

There are others, such as theater, where a single modality often does not dominate. It is long established by scholars and practitioners that theater engages visual, auditory, and kinesthetic modalities, often in nearly equal measure (Bowell & Heap, 2010; Harrington, 2018; Jensen, 2008; Toivanen, Mikkola, & Ruismäki, 2012).

In my work with arts educators over many years, I have observed time and again that, for those art forms that are associated with one primary learning modality, arts educators tend to privilege the learning modality that dominates their art form when they teach. When you stop and think about it, this is not surprising. After all, arts educators are artists as well as educators. As artists, they are accustomed to making art in their disciplines and engaging their art form's dominant modality to do so. Dance educators are dancers who traffic in how people move. Music educators are musicians who traffic in what people hear. Visual arts educators are visual artists who traffic in what people see.

As educators, arts educators nurture the artistry of their students.

- Dance educators help their students execute, analyze, create, and manipulate movements.
- Music educators help their students execute, analyze, create, and manipulate sound.
- Visual arts educators help their students execute, analyze, create, and manipulate what they see.

It is therefore not surprising that dance educators tend to teach with the kinesthetic modality, that music educators tend to teach with the auditory modality, and that visual arts educators tend to teach with the visual modality.

At the same time, however, bringing the commonly understood ideas about learning modalities to arts education reminds us to be mindful to expand the range of learning modalities that we employ in our teaching and that we engage in our students. To reach every learner, especially those who do not learn best in the modality that dominates our art form, it is incumbent on us to employ multiple learning modalities when we teach. Furthermore, when it comes to accessible arts education, there is one learning modality that rises far above the others: the visual modality. I explore the visual modality in greater detail in chapter 5 (page 143).

Engaging multiple modalities in arts learning settings might look something like the following. An elementary school art class is studying patterns. The teacher sets up a series of stations around the classroom with activities that provide students with different ways to explore and learn about patterns. At one station, students choose a type of pattern out of a hat (AAB, ABA, AABB, ABAC, and so on) and then use colored pencils, markers, and crayons to draw groups of shapes and symbols based on that type of pattern. At a second station, photographs of several naturally occurring patterns have been compiled on worksheets, and students use markers to label and circle the patterns they find on the worksheets. Teams of students at a third station create a series of movements that demonstrate patterns of various types. Using iPads, students at a fourth station create and record patterns of sounds in GarageBand (www.apple.com/mac/garageband).

As another example, a community band is rehearsing a new piece that includes a passage with very challenging rhythms. The conductor leads the students in several activities to help them learn, understand, and master the rhythms. The students:

- Walk around the room to a steady beat and clap the rhythms
- Stand still and clap the rhythms
- Use the rhythm syllable system of *du* and *du-de* to speak the rhythms
- Create their own notation system to draw the rhythms on pieces of paper
- Sing their parts with the correct rhythms
- Write the rhythms in musical notation

As part of a unit on character study, students in middle school drama are preparing monologues they will perform for the class at the end of the semester. They are given a series of assignments to complete along the way, including the following.

- Drawing a picture of their character

- Creating a paper doll of their character in costume and painting it
- Experimenting with different voices for their character by making audio recordings of their performances of the monologue in three possible voices, then writing a short essay about which voice they chose to use in their final performance and why
- Experimenting with different ways their character might walk by making video recordings of themselves walking in three different ways for the character, then writing a short essay about which walk they chose to use in their final performance and why
- Experimenting with different gestures their character might use by making video recordings of themselves performing the monologue with different gestures, then writing a short essay about which gestures they chose to use in their final performance and why

Learning Modalities Beyond the Big Three

During the pandemic, educators engaged in new ways of teaching and learning by necessity, as their in-person lessons, classes, and rehearsals all transitioned to online formats. Suddenly, we were striving to reach our students in new platforms that were not designed for our classes or our learning activities. Looking back on that time, I am amazed by the incredible resilience and ingenuity educators brought to the challenges of a global pandemic. We were all forced to reckon with teaching within the constraints of technology, which stifles the humanity of our teaching, our connections with our students, and our students' connections with each other and with their learning.

My experiences as an arts educator finding my way to teach in remote formats sparked my thinking about teaching, learning, and where and how they can take place. This led me to expand the notion of learning modalities beyond the big three of visual, auditory, and kinesthetic. I found myself making up names for other ways people might learn best, based on many conversations over a period of decades. Consider the following four new learning modalities I identified during the pandemic.

1. **Experiential:** Some people have told me they learn best when they have a direct experience with whatever it is they are learning. For example, they can attend a series of classes about sailing, but they don't feel they have really learned how to sail until they are in a real sailboat on the water, and they need to go from point A to point B.

   The experiential learning modality is woven deeply into the fabric of arts education. Arts education, by its very nature, usually involves direct experiences with creating the arts and responding to the arts. Students who learn best through direct experience have come to the right place in their arts learning settings, where they have opportunities to draw, paint, sculpt, sketch, dance, move, act, sing, play instruments, write, arrange, choreograph, create, compose, improvise, direct, produce, and much more. Direct experiences with and in the arts can often evoke emotions, challenge us to think, and remind us of what it means to be human.

   The experiential learning modality is also a key element of education in non-arts subjects. Students gain direct experience with their studies through projects, problem-solving sessions, field trips, and service learning, for just a few examples. By providing opportunities for students to learn through the experiential modality, educators can help their students understand the connections between the concepts and skills they are learning and their application to real-world situations.

   The experiential learning modality in an educational setting might look something like these examples.

   + A high school drama class presents a public performance of theatrical monologues. Students execute all the roles in the production, both on and off the stage. Students, sometimes individually and other times in teams, direct, produce, publicize, stage-manage, build sets, sew costumes, make props, sell tickets, and perform, all with guidance and support from their teacher. The students donate the proceeds from the performance to a local charity of their choice.

+ A fourth-grade science class plants and maintains a vegetable garden. The students begin by researching the best options for which crops to choose, based on the garden's location and soil type. Then, they create a plot for the setup of the garden. Next, the fourth graders procure the seeds and small plants and assemble the necessary tools for planting. Once they have planned the garden and prepared their materials, the students plant their crops. After planting is complete, the students create a watering and plant-food schedule so they can take turns attending to keeping the plants watered and nourished. When the crops eventually yield vegetables, the students donate them to a nearby food pantry.
+ A group of middle school students would like to start a school newspaper. The students engage in a monthlong learning exchange with a middle school student-newspaper team in another school district. Each student is assigned a mentor from the other district. The mentor shows their mentee how they do their jobs and explains what their role is like. The students get the opportunity to try out these roles with their partners' assistance. After having this hands-on experience with the students in the other school district, the middle schoolers begin to write, produce, and publish their own school newspaper.

2. **Social:** Some people have told me they learn best when they have the opportunity to discuss what they are learning with others. For example, they might read a book about how to manage their investments, but they won't truly know how to manage their investments until they talk about what they read with other people. It's through these conversations that they will come to know and understand investing.

The social learning modality in an educational setting might look something like these examples.

+ An elementary school dance class has just completed an activity where groups of students created and performed a sequence of movements that incorporated three vertical levels: up high, at waist level, and on the floor. The class is divided into groups of four students, and the groups are asked to assess their choreography's strengths and weaknesses and discuss what they learned from the activity.
+ Before the high school language arts class reads a play out loud, their teacher engages the students in a discussion of the text. Students identify the key themes of the play and how they are communicated in the script. With their teacher's guidance, each student explores the ways their character relates to the play's overarching themes.
+ In a group mural project, middle school art students work with each other to plan and execute the mural. Their teacher has provided them with a step-by-step guide for the project, which includes topics for discussion for each group meeting and a list of decisions that the group must make about the mural before they can submit their proposed mural for teacher approval.

3. **Explorational:** I have heard from some individuals that the best way for them to learn something is by investigating it on their own—by tinkering, trying things, and seeing how they work. For example, an explorational learner would come to learn a new software platform by diving in and exploring it on their own, as opposed to someone like me, who would read the manual first. Reading a manual doesn't help them learn the software; rather, exploring the software on their own is the best way for them to learn it.

   The explorational learning modality in an educational setting might look something like these examples.

+ Students in a middle school social studies class are learning about U.S. history in the 1970s. Their teacher has asked them to create a slideshow that presents the major events of that decade in chronological order using web-based research and YouTube videos. Students are required to share citations of the resources they used in their slideshows.
+ Students in a high school music composition class will use notation software for the first time to write down their compositions. The teacher provides them with copies of two musical notation software programs: MuseScore (www.musescore.com) and Sibelius (www.avid.com/sibelius). The students experiment with both platforms, choose one to use for their compositions, and share their compositions written with the software, along with an explanation of the reasons for their choice of platform.
+ Elementary-aged students in a community visual arts class are working with papier-mâché for the first time. Rather than demonstrate how to use this new medium, the teacher asks the students to experiment with papier-mâché and to make note of what they learn about the technique for using this medium. Students share how they experimented and the lessons they learned, and the teacher compiles this information into a handout as a reference for the class.

4. **Instructional:** I have heard from some people that they feel they have really learned something when they can teach it to someone else. For example, an instructional learner would know they have truly mastered the complexities of the game of bridge when they can teach someone else how to play it, and that person plays it successfully. For the instructional learner, understanding the rules of bridge, and even playing bridge themselves, pales in comparison to teaching someone else to play bridge when it comes to truly knowing the game.

The instructional learning modality in an educational setting might look something like these examples.

- Fourth-grade clarinet students in their beginner band group class have just learned how to assemble the instrument. Their teacher divides the class into pairs. In those pairs, the students are asked to teach each other how to put together the clarinet, starting with one student acting as the "teacher" and the other acting as the "student." Then the students switch roles so that both members of the duo have the opportunity to teach and to learn with each other.
- A theater teacher begins his high school theater class by leading the students in warm-up activities where the students engage in physical and vocal exercises. After a few weeks, he asks the students to create and facilitate their own warm-ups. Students are asked to share how they designed each warm-up and the intention of the warm-up and to reflect on the warm-up's effectiveness.
- Third graders are working on memorizing their spelling words for the week. Two days before their spelling test, the teacher asks the students to work in groups of four where they will quiz each other on their spelling words. She encourages the students to offer the hints and tricks they use to help their classmates spell the words correctly.

As I noted at the outset of this section, I made up and named these additional learning modalities on my own. This process was based not on systematic research but rather on my conversations with many people over a period of several decades. One or more of the additional learning modalities I made up may ring true for you and may jibe with either how you learn or how someone you know describes how they learn best. And one, two, or all of them may not reflect your understanding or experience. Certainly, if you were to make up your own additional learning modalities, they would be different from mine.

In the Artist's Words

I think I've just learned about myself. I'm not the type of artist that can just make things in isolation. I really need to be talking with people, seeing other work, and experiencing other projects, and I think there are also really amazing cross-disciplinary things that happen. There's a really amazing disability dance world here and seeing, you know, for example, description in dance performance and being like, "How would that relate to that description of static images?" or things like that, it's just, yeah, really fruitful. (Cowley Ford, 2023)

—**Finnegan Shannon**, artist

As we strive to make education more accessible for all students, we can—and should—expand our thinking about how people learn best and what effective teaching can be, beyond the frame of the big three learning modalities (visual, auditory, kinesthetic). The enterprise of learning and teaching is far more complex and multilayered than what can be captured in a three-part framework. To make education more accessible, we must broaden our understanding of learning modalities to make space for and validate the richness of the wide array of ways that people learn. It then follows naturally that we need to expand the ways we teach to forge meaningful, effective connections with as many ways that people learn as possible.

Having said all of this, it is important to highlight that the framework of the big three learning modalities has had a powerful influence on education and has served teachers well for decades. The fact that the big three is widely understood by so many educators today—and that it is generally accepted among educators that engaging more than one of the big three learning modalities makes for more effective teaching—is a testament to the framework's power. Without the big three framework, there may not have been any understanding of the value of teaching using more than one learning modality. The big three paved the way for educators to think more broadly about what a learning modality is and what learning modalities do mean and can mean for teachers and students.

Figure 4.1 illustrates how educators can plan to engage multiple learning modalities. In this example, a middle school general music class is learning about popular song form (verse-chorus-verse-chorus-bridge-verse-chorus).

Concept or Skill: Popular Song Form (Verse-Chorus-Verse-Chorus-Bridge-Verse-Chorus)	
Visual	Students label the sections of popular song form on lyric sheets and on sheet music.
Auditory	Students listen to songs in popular song form and raise their hands or hold up a sign as instructed (every time they hear the verse, the chorus, or the bridge).
Kinesthetic	Students create and demonstrate choreography that demonstrates the three sections (one sequence for the verse, one for the chorus, and one for the bridge) and perform it with a recording of the song.
Experiential	Students sing and play songs in popular song form.
Social	Students bring in recordings of songs in popular song form, play them for each other, and discuss them in groups.
Explorational	Before they learn what popular song form is, students try to derive popular song form by listening to songs and figuring it out on their own.
Instructional	Students teach each other what popular song form is and how to recognize it in songs they hear.
Other (Specify)	

FIGURE 4.1: Engaging multiple learning modalities—Middle school general music lesson on popular song form.

*Visit **go.SolutionTree.com/differentiatedinstruction** for a free reproducible version of this figure.*

Figure 4.2 provides an example of planning for multiple learning modalities for a high school social studies class that is learning about ancient Egypt.

Concept or Skill: Ancient Egypt	
Visual	Students bring in and share pictures they find in magazines or online that illustrate ancient Egypt. Students create visual representations (drawings, paintings, sculptures, collages, electronic media, and so on) of ancient Egypt based on what they have learned.
Auditory	Students listen to examples of ancient Egyptian music and contemporary Egyptian music and discuss their similarities and differences. Students listen to examples of ancient Egyptian music and discuss how what they hear may have influenced music they know.
Kinesthetic	Using YouTube videos and other online sources, students learn some common ancient Egyptian dance moves and sequences. They create and perform their own choreography using the moves and sequences they have learned.
Experiential	Students go on a field trip to an ancient Egypt exhibit at a local museum and engage in hands-on activities.
Social	Students conduct independent research into an aspect of ancient Egyptian culture and share what they have learned in group discussions.
Explorational	At the start of the unit, students search online for information about ancient Egypt and share what they found.
Instructional	Students quiz one another about vocabulary and concepts they have learned about ancient Egypt.
Other (Specify)	

FIGURE 4.2: Engaging multiple learning modalities—High school social studies lesson on ancient Egypt.

The wide range of ways in which people learn demands that teachers activate—and think broadly about—a wide range of ways of teaching. Multiple learning modalities is one framework we can use to expand the ways we teach. A second—and related—framework is to increase the range of pedagogical approaches we utilize with our students.

A Wide Range of Pedagogical Approaches

There are long-standing traditions in the ways the arts are taught in any culture, with roots that stretch back for generations. In the United States, Western traditions—and, in many cases, Western classical traditions—reign supreme in arts education. Think about the private piano teachers from the professional development workshop at the beginning of this chapter who were holding on to the traditions of what a private piano lesson looks like and were resistant to strategies that would mean stepping away from those traditions in their teaching.

Many—if not most—of us received our arts education and training within one or more of those traditions. That was certainly the case for me. The voice lessons and piano lessons I took for many years were all conducted in traditional ways that look and feel just like voice and piano lessons have looked and felt for generations: My activities were limited to standing and singing (in the voice lessons) or sitting and playing the piano (in the piano lessons). The same was true of my collegiate studies at the conservatory I attended. For example, the harmony course I took was steeped in the Western classical music tradition, and it was taught using the same materials and pedagogy that have been used to teach harmony courses for generations. Numerous scholars have observed that the curriculum in today's collegiate music programs looks very much the same as it did more than 150 years ago (Bates, 2023; Bernard, 2016; Burton, 2011; Conway, 2020; Jones, 2012; Kratus, 2007, 2009, 2011, 2015; Palmer & de Quadros, 2012; Randles, 2015).

Long-standing traditions also persist in the ways that non-arts subjects are taught—traditions that, like those in the arts, are culturally bound and have been around for generations (Teschers, Neuhaus, & Vogt, 2024; Wyss, Kocher, & Baer, 2017). When I reflect on my own non-arts education, for example, certain indelible images and memories come to mind that illustrate how some of those traditions played out in my public schooling in the 1970s: rows of chairs and desks, worksheet assignments, and memorization homework, for just a few examples.

However, as I mentioned earlier in this chapter, the stranglehold that these traditions have over the educational enterprise functions as a barrier to making education truly accessible for all students. Students who don't learn best with the traditional pedagogical approach may not have access to their education. Reducing or removing this barrier requires educators to engage a wide range of pedagogical approaches that extends far beyond the traditions and meets students where they are.

Engaging a wide range of pedagogical approaches might look something like the following.

- Students in a children's theater program are working on two-person scenes. In addition to the traditional approaches of memorizing their lines, rehearsing with their scene partners, and performing their scenes for the class, the students engage in other activities, including writing journal entries about the ways they empathize with their character and with their scene partner's character, discussing how their personal experiences relate to the situation of the scene, writing and speaking the subtext of every line in the scene, improvising different lines in the same situation as the scene, directing scenes performed by other students, improvising a new scene with the same two characters, and much more.
- Students in a middle school general music class are learning the chromatic scale. In addition to the traditional approaches of playing the chromatic scale on an instrument and writing

the chromatic scale in conventional musical notation, the students engage in other activities, including listening to music and raising their hands when they hear the chromatic scale, finding recordings of pieces of music that contain the chromatic scale and bringing them to class, explaining what the chromatic scale is to their classmates, and identifying and correcting errors in written and performed chromatic scale examples that have been altered to include mistakes, for just a few examples.

- Students in an elementary school mathematics class are working on long division. In addition to the traditional approaches of completing long-division problems on worksheets, the students engage in other activities, including creating their own word problems that require long division for their classmates to solve, correcting teacher-provided long-division errors on the board, making a list of practical applications of long division in everyday life, demonstrating long division for one another using manipulatives, and writing out the list of steps for solving a long-division problem.
- Students in a high school dance class are being introduced to tap dancing. In addition to the traditional approaches of watching their teacher demonstrate and then trying the steps on their own or mirroring their teacher and dancing along with them, the students engage in other activities, including clapping their hands to the rhythms that their feet will eventually tap as a way to learn choreography, using gestures to correspond with different tap step sequences and playing out a longer dance with gestures, watching and analyzing videos of tap dance performances, listening to audio recordings of tap dancing and trying to discern the steps, and choreographing their own tap dance sequences and teaching them to the other students, among others.

Educators can use figure 4.3 (page 136) to plan for engaging a range of pedagogical approaches, using the children's theater program example.

Concept or Skill	Possible Pedagogical Approaches
Two-Person Scenes	Students memorize their lines, rehearse with their scene partners, and perform their scenes for the class.
	Students write journal entries about the ways they empathize with their character and with their scene partner's character.
	Students discuss how their personal experiences relate to the situation of the scene.
	Students write out and speak the subtext of every line in the scene.
	Students improvise different lines in the same situation as the scene.
	Students direct scenes that other students perform.
	Students improvise a new scene with the same two characters.

FIGURE 4.3: Planning for a range of pedagogical approaches—Children's theater.

Visit ***go.SolutionTree.com/differentiatedinstruction*** *for a free reproducible version of this figure.*

Figure 4.4 uses the preceding elementary mathematics class example. All of this makes logical sense: Educational experiences can be more accessible to every student, no matter how they learn best and no matter whether or how they can benefit from supports, if educators widen the range of ways in which they teach. Engaging multiple learning modalities and activating a wide range of pedagogical approaches serve to reduce and remove barriers to learning that might be at play, thereby opening up opportunities for more students to learn.

Concept or Skill	Possible Pedagogical Approaches
Long Division	Students complete long-division problems on worksheets.
	Students create their own word problems that require long division for their classmates to solve.
	Students correct teacher-provided long-division errors on the board.
	Students make a list of practical applications of long division in everyday life.
	Students demonstrate long division for each other using manipulatives.
	Students write out the steps for solving a long-division problem.

FIGURE 4.4: Planning for a range of pedagogical approaches—Long division.

This is not to say there is no place at all for the traditional ways of teaching and learning, or that we should abandon any and all connections to those traditions. The traditional approaches have worked—and can work—for some students, and they have stood the test of time. However, they are just the beginning. Put slightly differently, the traditional approaches should not be the only ways in which students are taught; rather, they should be among many learning modalities and pedagogical approaches that educators engage and employ.

It is also important to understand and recognize that the traditional approaches to teaching and learning are embedded in particular cultures and time periods. The underlying assumptions about education that were widely accepted in those cultures and time periods influence other aspects of the traditional teaching and learning approaches that merit critical examination and reflection. These include notions of the power dynamic between teacher and student (chapter 2, page 57) and understandings regarding what content is legitimate for study, for just a couple of examples. Rather than accepting and revering tradition for tradition's sake, today's educators have the opportunity to uncover and interrogate these and other dynamics that play out in the traditional approaches to education. We must determine for ourselves how our teaching practice today relates to, incorporates, builds on, or resists those dynamics.

Takeaways

While educational traditions have served us well for generations, many of them are grounded in very particular notions of what teaching and learning look like and how they take place. As we have come to understand and appreciate the wide variety of ways students learn, it is incumbent on educators to develop an equally wide—if not wider—variety of ways to teach to reach every student (Bernard, 2016). The habits of mind and pedagogical strategies of accessible arts education can help arts educators imagine, explore, and enact the educational process in ways that extend beyond the traditional models so that every student can engage and learn meaningfully, no matter how they learn best.

More specifically, the expansion of our conception of teaching and learning undergirds the concepts and strategies in this chapter and the ways they relate to accessibility. As we open up pathways for more students to engage, participate, and learn in more meaningful ways, we reduce and remove barriers, making our teaching more accessible.

In the Artist's Words

I had a wonderful, amazing mentor when I was student teaching and I learned so, so much from her. She helped me devise some of these strategies. For example, we have them sit at the tables so that you can hear the chairs scraping across the floor to indicate when they're standing or sitting. If you hear too much noise and they're not singing, that's how you know they're not paying attention. When they get like this, you know to bring them back to center. I'm just paying more attention to things like this as a blind teacher. People say things like, "Your senses are heightened!" Well, it's because I use them. It's not necessarily because they're making up for lack of sight—it's that I don't have sight so I'm using my other senses. If you were to put on a blindfold and just sit there and listen, you would be able to hear more and identify more than you think. (Bernard, 2022a)

—**Precious Perez**, singer, songwriter, author, and disability advocate

Now, today I find learning music is just second nature to me. So, I sit at the piano and learn vocal scores and it doesn't impact on my autism at all. But, when it involves large stage productions, this is where it starts to get a bit trickier for me, especially opera productions, where there is lots of complicated staging. So, learning the operatic scores is fine, anything to do with the music side of production is easy, but the staging is another matter. Because, I struggle with the stage director's instructions, however, this has clearly never stopped me. Yeah, and I have managed very early on in my career to get around this problem by drawing colored pictures of every scene in an opera, for me to be able to follow the stage direction. So, I see all the staging in color. For example, I give the characters in the operas colors instead of using their names, and stage left is blue and stage right is pink. And so, I have all these colored pictures I have drawn on A3-size pieces of paper, and they look very similar to children's drawings. In fact, I was singing at one opera company and I decided to be brave and put the pictures up in the greenroom, as I thought this might help me follow what I'm doing, but the director came in and saw them and said, "Can someone please remove all the children's drawings from the wall?" You know, because I've always hidden it from other cast members, but today I'm just more open about that now.

—Sophia Grech, opera singer
and autism ambassador

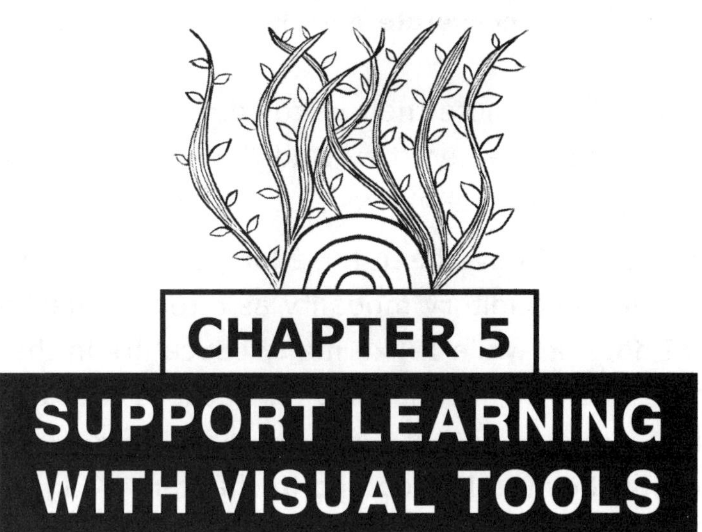

CHAPTER 5

SUPPORT LEARNING WITH VISUAL TOOLS

I would describe myself as an extremely auditory person. I remember what I hear quite vividly and for a long time. And when words are in the mix—like song lyrics or something a person says—what I hear becomes deeply ingrained in my memory. This has served me well as a musician because remembering what I hear helps me learn and transcribe music quickly, as well as incorporate what others have played into my improvised solos.

I easily and regularly engage the auditory modality as part of my processes of reading, writing, thinking, learning, and memorizing. When I read, I hear myself saying the words in my mind's ear. The same is true when I write: As I produce the words on the page or screen, I hear myself saying them. I hear my voice saying words, sentences, paragraphs, and even pages when I am thinking through ideas, learning something new, forming an argument, or planning a complex event or program. When I want to remember something—the name of a person I just met, a shopping list, a time-sensitive task, driving directions, or the name and address of a restaurant, for just a few examples—I say it out loud. I am wired for the auditory modality. It comes naturally, and it works for me.

I often warn other people, jokingly, that they do not want to get into an argument with me because (much to the chagrin of those who do) I will quote their words directly back to them, and I will even remember when they said the words, what they and I were wearing, and where we were at the time.

I am aware, and I have been for a long time, that most people do not engage the auditory modality as often, as naturally, or as deeply as I do. And while I, like many educators in the United States, have been well acquainted for decades with the generally accepted understanding that effective teaching requires engaging multiple modalities (as I discussed in chapter 4, page 115), it was not until I developed the tools, strategies, frameworks, and habits of mind of accessible arts education that I fully comprehended that the auditory modality is not the most fruitful teaching and learning modality when it comes to making educational experiences accessible for all students. That distinction belongs to the visual modality.

This chapter explores the effectiveness of the visual modality in making arts education accessible for all students. It begins by examining the unique aspects of the visual modality, followed by a discussion of the ways those aspects contribute to increasing the accessibility of arts education experiences. The next section of the chapter features specific strategies for teachers to utilize visuals of various kinds, and for various purposes, in arts education settings. The chapter concludes with a discussion of accessible arts education for students who have challenges processing visual information.

The Unique Aspects of the Visual Modality

The visual modality is uniquely invaluable when it comes to making arts lessons, classes, and rehearsals more accessible for all students. Unlike the auditory and kinesthetic modalities, the visual modality functions in two ways simultaneously: both as a modality for teaching and learning and as a support for our students. In the latter function, the visual modality makes learning and engagement more accessible, as it helps students with the processes of taking in, understanding, manipulating, and remembering information, ideas, skills, and instructions (Sam & Autism Focused Intervention Resources and Modules, 2016b; Steinbrenner et al., 2020).

The uniqueness of the visual modality stems from its relationship with time. Kinesthetic and auditory experiences are bound by time in ways that visual experiences are not. What does this mean, what does it look like in education, and how does it relate to accessibility?

A kinesthetic experience takes place, and then it concludes. In educational settings, teachers demonstrate what they are teaching by moving their bodies, and their students execute movements for a period of time. When the time period is over, the kinesthetic experience has ended. The kinesthetic experience is temporary and bounded by time.

Similarly, an auditory experience occurs, and then it is over. Educators demonstrate by making sounds and their students create sounds for a period of time. When the time period concludes, the auditory experience has finished. The auditory experience is temporary and bounded by time.

We can create records of kinesthetic and auditory experiences, but they are mere documents of the experiences, not the experiences themselves. Put another way, it is possible to video-record teachers and students as they dance and move, and it is possible to audio-record teachers and students as they speak, play, and sing. Educators and their students can watch the video recording or listen to the audio recording after having danced, moved, spoken, played, or sung. But watching or listening to a recording is not the same thing as actually dancing, moving, speaking, playing, or singing. Watching or listening to a recording is not the experience itself; rather, it is an interaction with a record of the experience.

When teachers employ the visual modality, they use visual tools, such as text or images on the whiteboard or projected on a screen, word walls, signs and symbols on classroom materials, props, and so on. Unlike the temporary, time-bound nature of kinesthetic and audio experiences that take place through those learning modalities, the visual tools that educators use stick around long after the teacher has pointed to them, explained them, or displayed them. They are not temporary. The fact that visual tools last longer than students' in-the-moment experience with them gives visual tools an additional function: They become supports for students who need them (Center for Autism and Related Disabilities, n.d.; Hodgdon, 2023; Kosky Deskin, 2013; McVay, Wilson, & Chiotti, 2003). (For more visual strategies for autism, visit www.usevisualstrategies.com.)

The Visual Modality and Accessible Arts Education

When educators utilize visual tools in their teaching, they are engaging the visual modality *and* providing supports that make their teaching more accessible. Because visual supports are not time limited and stick around, students can use them long after the teacher introduces or displays them. Providing these supports reduces and removes barriers for students, increasing their access to their educational experience.

As is the case with all accessible arts education strategies, many, many students—not just those with a diagnosed disability—can benefit from visual tools as a means of support, including the following, for just some examples.

- Students who need extra time to process visual information
- Students who need extra time to process auditory information
- Students who are less familiar with the material being studied
- Students who are struggling to develop their skills
- Students who are distracted
- Students who have difficulty focusing their attention or who are not sure where to focus their attention
- Students whose senses are overwhelmed

- Students who have difficulty holding information in their short-term memory
- Students who feel anxious and are having a difficult time concentrating
- Students for whom English is not their first language
- Students with hearing loss or who are deaf
- Students who wish to double-check their work

Visual tools can be an extremely potent source of support for students. When I teach undergraduate and graduate courses and provide professional development about accessible arts education, I emphasize the power of visual tools and urge preservice and in-service educators to expand their use of visual tools in their teaching. Many of these individuals reach out to me weeks or months later to share that they have incorporated more visual tools into their teaching practice based on our work together, and they have already seen a noticeable difference in their students' participation and learning as a result. Increasing the amount and types of visual tools that we utilize in our teaching can have a powerful positive impact on the accessibility of our classes, lessons, and ensemble rehearsals.

Strategies for Employing Visuals in Educational Settings

Educators can employ visuals as tools for teaching, communicating information, providing instructions, and structuring independent student work. As one example of engaging visuals as tools for teaching, imagine an elementary general music teacher is leading a lesson on the distinction between quarter notes and eighth notes in simple rhythmic figures. He provides several visual tools as he teaches the lesson, including the following.

- Chart paper with both note values written in musical notation, each labeled "quarter note" or "eighth note" with text

- A slide that contains quarter notes and eighth notes in different configurations in eight measures in 4/4 time projected on the SMART Board
- A poster with a circle (to represent a measure of 4/4 time) that is divided into quarters (to illustrate quarter notes)
- A poster with a circle (to represent a measure of 4/4 time) that is divided into eighths (to illustrate eighth notes)
- Handouts of simple songs that the students know written out in musical notation, all of which include only quarter notes and eighth notes
- Demonstrations that the teacher gives in front of the class where the teacher claps short rhythmic phrases made up of only quarter notes and eighth notes

Let's consider an example of what it might look like to provide multiple forms of visuals to communicate information. A dance teacher introduces her middle school–aged students to new choreography with several visuals, including written-out prompt words for each movement (such as step, touch, walk, turn), diagrams posted at the front of the room that show exactly how the students will move through space, cutouts of feet placed on the classroom floor, a video of the choreography being executed, and her own demonstration and modeling in front of the class.

What might it look like to use visuals to provide instructions? A middle school science teacher uses multiple forms of visuals to communicate the guidelines for a project where students are to conduct an experiment and create a lab report. The instructions for the assignment are written in text on the whiteboard in the classroom. In a handout, students receive a checklist of the components for the assignment and the rubric that the teacher will use to assess the assignment. Displayed prominently in the classroom is a large piece of chart paper with the instructions written out with symbols to represent each guideline for the assignment. The teacher shows a short video of an example of a completed assignment that meets all the criteria, and the video includes captions that point out each component of the assignment as it is represented on the video.

Incorporating visuals into the structure of independent-work settings can look like students in a community creative writing class working on independent short story projects. Their teacher has informed them that they will spend thirty minutes of class time writing; then the class will come together as a group so that they can share their stories with each other. The teacher uses visuals to structure the students' independent work and empower them to manage their time, including the following.

- The teacher projects a digital timer counting down from thirty minutes on the whiteboard so students who recognize this form of timekeeping will know how much time remains.
- The teacher projects a video of an analog clock ticking back from thirty minutes on the whiteboard so students who are familiar with this form of timekeeping will know how much time remains.
- The teacher projects a video of a sand timer that empties over thirty minutes on the whiteboard so students for whom this form of timekeeping is helpful will know how much time remains.
- The teacher deposits a piece of green construction paper on each student's table at the start of the time period to represent that it is time to go. Halfway through the time period, the teacher takes away the green paper and deposits a piece of yellow construction paper on each table to communicate that half of their work time has expired. Five minutes before their work time is scheduled to end, the teacher removes the yellow construction paper and deposits a piece of red construction paper on each table to signal that there are five minutes left of their work time.

Using the example of the creative writing class, figure 5.1 (page 150) shows how educators can brainstorm and plan for visual tools.

Lesson or Unit: Short Story Projects	
Visuals for Teaching	• Graphic organizer to help students plan their short stories • Drawing of the plot of a sample short story
Visuals to Communicate Information	• Handout with the elements of short stories • Sample short story with each element highlighted
Visuals to Provide Instructions	• Short story assignment guidelines on a piece of chart paper • Handout with a checklist for the short story assignment • Handout with a rubric that the teacher will use to assess the short story assignments
Visuals for Independent Work	• Digital timer countdown projected on the board • Analog clock countdown projected on the board • Actual sand timer at the front of the classroom • Three pieces of paper the teacher hands out (green at the start of the time frame, yellow at the midpoint, and red five minutes before the end of the time frame)

FIGURE 5.1: Planning for visual tools.

*Visit **go.SolutionTree.com/differentiatedinstruction** for a free reproducible version of this figure.*

The strategies for using visuals in the classroom are neither radical nor revolutionary; however, their impact on student engagement, participation, and learning can be surprisingly powerful. Educators who step up their use of these tools are often amazed at their potency, both as teaching and learning modalities and as supports for students. Visual tools can be the key that unlocks accessibility for many students, opening up doors that had been barriers and making new learning pathways possible.

Personalized Visual Tools for Students Who Are Blind or Low Vision

For some individuals who are blind or low vision, customizing visual tools can make them more accessible. These students may benefit from using visual tools that are personalized in terms of their size, typeface, and color contrast.

Increasing the size of visual tools can make them more accessible and more effective. One of the most common ways to personalize visual tools is by increasing the size of the typeface in materials that are either projected on a screen or printed on paper. Simply making words, symbols, pictures, graphics, musical notation, and other visual information physically larger can increase the effectiveness of visual tools for some individuals based on how their brain processes visual information. Through consultations with the student and with the special education team, teachers can determine the point size for typefaces and the sizes of images and icons that are most effective for a particular individual (ADA Site Compliance, 2023; American Foundation for the Blind, n.d.; Willings, n.d.).

Using certain typefaces in visual tools increases their accessibility and effectiveness. According to ADA Site Compliance (2023), the following sans serif typefaces—that is, typefaces whose letters don't have extensions, or *serifs*, at the end of letter strokes—are more accessible because they are easier to read and decode.

- Helvetica
- Verdana
- Tahoma

In addition, using roman font (rather than italics) and using both upper and lower cases (rather than small caps or all caps) can make visual tools more accessible for students with low vision (ADA Site Compliance, 2023; Willings, n.d.). Spacing is another important consideration, as it can be difficult to read words and lines of text that are closer together. Helvetica, Verdana, Tahoma, and other sans serif typefaces are considered accessible in part because the spacing between letters within words is wide. Attending to spacing between the lines of text is another way to increase accessibility, with a line spacing of 1.5 most commonly recommended (ADA Site Compliance, 2023; American Foundation for the Blind, n.d.; Willings, n.d.).

Creating materials with high color contrasts can make them more accessible and more effective. Carmen Willings (n.d.), in her article for Teaching Students With Visual Impairments, a resource website for educators, recommends the highest possible color contrast in visual materials and supports to ensure maximum accessibility: "Use light (white or light yellow) letters on a dark (black or dark colored) background or dark letters on a light or white background." In her guide for teachers titled "High Contrast and Low Vision," Veronica Lewis (2024) echoes this recommendation and provides specific examples of effective and ineffective color contrasts for visual tools so that educators can see exactly what high and low color contrasts look like.

Auditory Supports and Tactile Tools

For some individuals who are blind or low vision, visual tools may not be compatible with the ways that their brains process visual information. These students may benefit from supports that are provided either by pairing the visual modality with other modalities or by using other modalities instead of the visual modality.

Pairing visual tools and materials with auditory supports can be an effective way to increase the accessibility of visual elements for students who are blind or low vision. A few examples include referring to students by their names when addressing them, reading aloud and describing what is written on the board, using auditory cues for transitions or the amount of time that remains to work on a particular task or assignment, and creating digital materials that can be read by a screen reader on the student's computer or phone (Castellano, 2005; Perkins School for the Blind, n.d.; Student Disability Services, n.d.). When I had a blind student in my freshman seminar, his classmates volunteered to take turns providing audio descriptions for the videos they showed as part of their project presentations. The students took great pride in providing vivid and clear verbal accounts of what they saw on the screen, and the blind student was extremely pleased to have the opportunity to gain access to the visual aspects of the videos.

Utilizing tactile tools can also make learning more accessible for students who are blind or low vision. Tactile supports might include the use of braille as well as tactile graphics, which are specially designed images to be touched rather than viewed (Cushman, 2024; Perkins School for the Blind, n.d.; Tactile Graphics, n.d.). Other tactile supports can take the form of hands-on fine-motor activities (performed with or without assistance) that take place in class, such as creating shapes using clay or placing fingers on specific holes on the recorder (Perkins School for the Blind, n.d.; Student Disability Services, n.d.).

Takeaways

As someone who considers herself to be an extremely auditory person, I have come to appreciate the occasions in my life when visual tools have served and supported me well. One such occasion is when I am traveling in a country where a language other than English is spoken. I benefit greatly from visual tools (text, symbols, lip reading, pantomiming, and so on) to communicate with others, to understand signage, to order at a restaurant, and to use household appliances in an Airbnb, for just a few situations.

Although the visual modality is not my preferred modality personally, it has become the most significant teaching and learning modality that I use as an educator because of its dual functions as a modality and a support. Even though I teach music and music education, I have found that my teaching has become significantly more effective for all my students—whether in a graduate course or a kindergarten classroom—when I engage the visual modality. The visual tools I provide give my students additional supports that reduce and remove barriers to their learning, such as the need for additional processing time or challenges with paying attention and being distracted, for just a couple of examples. I implore you to consider, explore, and implement visual tools in your teaching whenever you can, with careful attention to those instances when visual tools alone may be insufficient for a particular student.

In the Artist's Words

I handle a lot of the visual stuff, the artwork, the outfits, and anything that you can see of Artio [the alt-rock quartet for which Rae is the front person]. It's either been done by me or has been designed or orchestrated or produced, I guess, visually by me. That's because I'm a very visual person, and when we write music, I can hear and see the music video. I know what the color scheme is going to be from picking the song, and it's not like a decompartmentalized process; it just is. It just happens. (Valentine, 2024)

—**Rae Brazill**, songwriter, performer, designer, and director

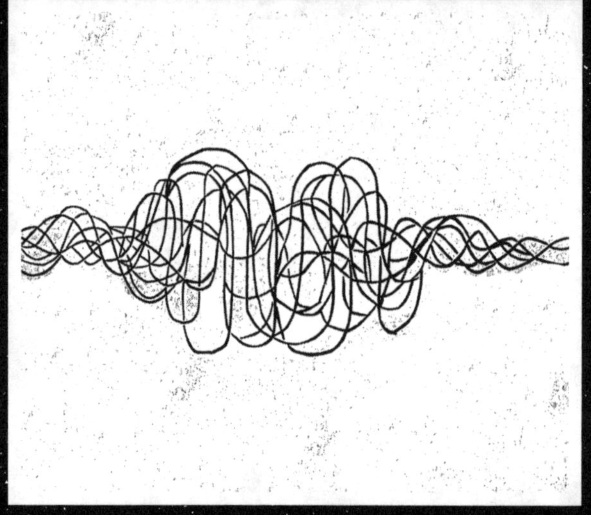

I don't really like loud sounds, and . . . everyone gives me grief about that, and they're all like, "But you're in a rock band?" I'm like, "Yeah, I'm aware of that. I am just a special little guy with special little allocations for me to do things." And like, when we're on tour, we have a policy that if there's going to be a loud noise, everyone has to shout, "Ears!" and then I'll cover my ears. Or, I won't be brought into the room until I have to be, and I'm essentially babysat on tour by people who understand what it is to be caring for an autistic person and facilitating an artist at the same time, and I'm very lucky that I have a team that is very inclusive of me and just accommodate me, which is great.

—Rae Brazill, songwriter, performer, designer, and director

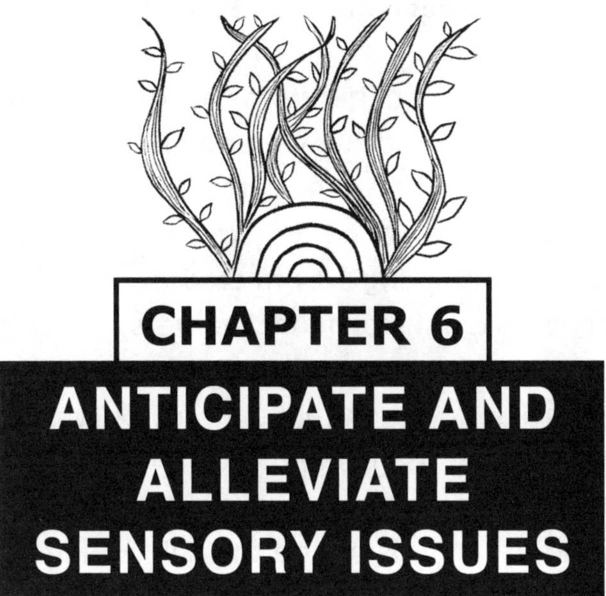

CHAPTER 6
ANTICIPATE AND ALLEVIATE SENSORY ISSUES

As I mentioned earlier, I wrote this book during my sabbatical leave. The first week of the sabbatical was bookended by sensory issues: one for me, and one for a music teacher at a professional development workshop that I was leading.

At six o'clock in the morning on the very first day of the sabbatical, I was abruptly and harshly awakened by the house-shakingly loud, aggressively high-pitched sound of the six hardwired smoke detectors in my home going off at once. The alarms sounded for forty-five seconds and then went silent. This auditory assault repeated every thirty minutes for the next two hours until I was able to locate the unit that was causing the issue and pull it out from the ceiling. Meanwhile, online research and a few phone calls revealed that (a) my house's interconnected smoke detectors are low voltage (which means they are not controlled by a single circuit breaker), and (b) their misbehavior that morning likely indicated it was time to replace them. An alarm specialist stopped by later in the day; confirmed that the smoke detectors had, in fact, reached the end of their working lives; and scheduled a time to install new units the following week.

I learned something valuable from this experience—something beyond my research about low-voltage interconnected smoke detectors. I learned that I am sensitive to extremely loud mechanical sounds. The sound the smoke alarms made was more than just loud and annoying—it affected my body and mind. I experienced classic fight-or-flight markers, including elevated heart rate, shallow breathing, higher body temperature, and constricted muscles. My cognitive experience was one of franticness. My disorganized thoughts gushed forth at breakneck speed. I was able to think only about shallow, immediate concerns. It took me two hours to locate and dismantle the culprit unit and end the cycle of alarms because I was not able to reason effectively.

At the end of the same week, I gave a professional development workshop at a local community music school. When I arrived and connected my computer to the projector in the recital hall, I noticed that the image on the screen was flickering, frequently disappearing and returning. The session organizers informed me that the projector was near the end of its life, and other presenters had experienced the same issues earlier that day.

I forged ahead and began the workshop, explaining to the attendees that I would try to use the projector, and they would receive copies of the slides after the session. Unfortunately, the machine's unpredictable behavior continued, and the projection of the slides was not reliable at all. I referred to text, graphics, or pictures that should have been visible on the slides, but the image on the screen was either absent altogether or flashing and impossible to read or understand. Furthermore, the projector could not support any of the video clips I had planned to show during the presentation—the display stuttered to the point that the recordings were not watchable. I asked the group whether I should continue to use the projector, and the attendees indicated I should. They wanted the option of seeing the slides, even intermittently, during the workshop.

About ten minutes later, I noticed that one teacher was shielding her eyes with her right hand, just like one would do to block the sun on a sunny day. At that point, I decided to disconnect my computer from the projector. I told the attendees I was going to do so, since the technical issues remained unresolved. As soon as the projector shut off, the teacher who had been covering her eyes removed her hand, sighed, and smiled at me.

After the session, she came up to me and said, "Thanks for going low-tech today. I couldn't look at that screen for another minute." She explained that when the image was flickering, she was unable to concentrate during the session and could not participate in the workshop. "I guess I'm really sensitive to flashing lights," she noted.

All of us continuously receive, process, and integrate sensory information. When doing so presents challenges, as it did for me with the sound of the smoke alarms and for the teacher with the flashing images from the projector, there may be an issue of some kind with sensory processing (Miller, Schoen, Mulligan, & Sullivan, 2017). Statistics indicate that sensory issues affect up to 30 percent of the population at large (Acevedo, 2025). Sensory issues are even more common among people with disabilities. Researchers have found that as many as 80 to 100 percent of people with autism, ADHD, prematurity, fetal alcohol syndrome, Down syndrome, and other diagnoses experience sensory processing issues (Kojovic, Ben Hadid, Franchini, & Schaer, 2019; Kong & Moreno, 2018; Miller et al., 2017).

This chapter provides strategies to help educators anticipate and alleviate sensory issues in teaching and learning settings. To lay the groundwork for these strategies, the next section considers a range of sensory issues and their implications for educators and students.

Sensory Issues

Research on the difficulties that people can encounter when they process sensory information was first shared in 1972 in occupational therapist and educational psychologist A. Jean Ayres's groundbreaking book *Sensory Integration and Learning Disorders*.

In this volume, Ayres presents the theoretical framework she developed, known as Sensory Integration theory. She also discusses the assessment of and treatments for children with sensory integration dysfunction. Early reception of Ayres's work sparked criticism from some occupational therapists and prompted extensive research into the nature, assessment, and treatment of sensory difficulties (Arendt, MacLean, & Baumeister, 1988; Cummins, 1991; Hoehn & Baumeister, 1994). The overwhelming majority of that research has corroborated and elaborated on Ayres's scholarship (Kilroy, Aziz-Zadeh, & Cermak, 2019; Steinbrenner et al., 2020). As a result, for more than two decades, Ayres's contributions to the field have been widely hailed as pioneering and tremendously influential in furthering the understanding, assessment, and treatment of sensory processing challenges (Omairi, Mailloux, Antoniuk, & Schaaf, 2022; Schaaf & Mailloux, 2015; Watling & Hauer, 2015).

SPOTLIGHT: SENSORY INTEGRATION THEORY

Grounded in rigorous neurological research and real-life occupational therapy practice with individuals with learning disabilities and behavioral challenges, Sensory Integration theory is considered by many scholars and researchers to have been ahead of its time when A. Jean Ayres first articulated it in 1972 (Lane et al., 2019).

Sensory Integration theory is based on the following key ideas (Collaborative for Leadership in Ayres Sensory Integration [CLASI], n.d.; Gasiewski & Weiss, 2022).

- The brain organizes and interprets sensory information.
- Humans require effective sensory organization to respond to sensory input appropriately and to function successfully.
- When sensory information is not organized effectively, it can lead to difficulties in learning, behavior, social participation, physical actions, and the performance of tasks.

Although more than fifty years have passed since Ayres developed Sensory Integration theory, its relevance and its widespread use as the basis for intervention continue to this day. To ensure the unique identity of the therapeutic strategies that Ayres developed back in the 1970s, Ayres Sensory Integration® was trademarked in 2007 (Gasiewski & Weiss, 2022), and Ayres's former students created CLASI to provide educational programs, workshops, mentorship, and professional certification for occupational therapists around the world (CLASI, n.d.).

Today's researchers and practitioners make a distinction between sensory sensitivity and sensory processing disorder. Sensory sensitivity is a trait, not a condition or disorder. Individuals who are sensory sensitive can benefit from an awareness of situations where sensory input may affect them and the recognition that they may need additional time to process sensory stimuli or information. By contrast, sensory processing disorder is a neurological condition that presents challenges to one's ability to receive, interpret, and respond to sensory input. These challenges disrupt the everyday lives of people with sensory processing disorder and could include feeling overwhelmed by one or more senses or feeling that sensory input is muted (Acevedo, 2025).

SPOTLIGHT: SENSORY PROCESSING DISORDER

In her highly influential book *Sensational Kids: Hope and Help for Children With Sensory Processing Disorder (SPD),* researcher and occupational therapist Lucy Jane Miller (2014) subdivides sensory processing disorder into three components: (1) sensory modulation disorder, (2) sensory discrimination disorder, and (3) sensory-based motor disorder. Researchers and practitioners continue to use this framework (Binder, 2021; Galiana-Simal et al., 2020; Whiting, Schoen, & Niemeyer, 2023).

Sensory modulation is a person's ability to respond to sensory stimuli in a way that matches the stimuli's intensity and nature. Difficulties in sensory modulation might take three forms.

1. Being overly responsive or sensitive to sensory stimuli
2. Being under-responsive or unable to respond to sensory stimuli
3. Craving or seeking sensory input

Sensory discrimination has to do with understanding the nature and intensity of sensory input. Instances of challenges with sensory discrimination might include having difficulty reaching into a bag and locating a set of keys without looking or not applying enough pressure with the hands to catch a ball.

Sensory-based motor disorder refers to movement-related sensory challenges, such as planning and organizing new movements; balancing, controlling, and stabilizing through movements; or determining the location of one's body in space when moving. Sensory-based motor challenges could manifest in poor balance, the appearance of floppy muscles, clumsiness, or trouble knowing what strokes to make on paper or how to hold a pencil when writing (Alta Pediatrics, n.d.; Kong & Moreno, 2018; Miller, 2014).

In educational settings, sensory issues can act as barriers that can interfere with student engagement, participation, and learning. For example, individuals who are sensory sensitive might have difficulty paying attention, concentrating, and thinking clearly and effectively when they are overwhelmed by sensory input. This could lead them to avoid learning situations, run away, or have a meltdown. People who seek sensory stimulation might encounter problems sitting still, feel compelled to touch people or textures, or misunderstand personal space in their interactions with others. This could cause them to fidget, reach out and touch other people and classroom items, or bump and crash into people and objects. In these ways and more, some learners who experience sensory issues might not be able to engage, participate, and learn effectively.

Sensory issues can occur in relation to seven senses: the five external senses (sight, hearing, touch, smell, and taste) and the two internal senses (vestibular and proprioceptive). The five external senses are the most familiar senses—the ones that people most often refer to when they speak about senses. However, the two internal senses are equally important and can often be at play when sensory issues arise. The *vestibular sense* has to do with balance and, more specifically, with the position of a person's head. While the physical mechanism involved with the vestibular sense is located in the inner ear, the felt experience of the vestibular sense manifests through a sense of balance and posture as well as through eye movements (Casale, Browne, Murray, & Gupta, 2025). The *proprioceptive sense* refers to how an individual understands the position of their body in space and the movements of their body, in ways beyond what they can sense visually. One common example of how proprioception works is when someone scratches an itch on their nose. The brain knows how to move the hand directly to the nose to scratch the itch, without needing to see the hand or the nose to do so (Cleveland Clinic, n.d.b).

Strategies to Reduce and Remove the Barrier of Sensory Issues in Educational Settings

By attending to and addressing sensory issues, educators can make their learning spaces and activities more accessible for all students. The strategies that follow are some effective ways teachers can inventory, analyze, and modulate the sensory aspects of the classroom environment and their planned learning activities.

Conducting a Comprehensive Sensory Audit of the Learning Environment

One of the most effective ways to anticipate and alleviate sensory issues in the teaching environment is to conduct a sensory audit. In this case, because the focus is on an external, physical space, only the five external senses are relevant. A sensory audit of the learning environment, then, is a structured inventory and analysis of a space through the lens of the external senses (sight, hearing, touch, smell, and taste). To conduct a sensory audit, a teacher walks through their space five times, each time focusing only on one external sense and the potential sensory issues that might arise. So, for example, the visual walkthrough would be an opportunity for the educator to examine and analyze all visual elements in the environment, with the aim of identifying any potential visual sensory issues that might arise. The auditory walkthrough would be a separate occasion that would focus on all auditory elements in the environment, and so on, for each of the five external senses. The walkthroughs can provide valuable information about potential sensory issues in the learning environment.

Figure 6.1 illustrates how an elementary visual arts teacher who shares her classroom with the music teacher might conduct a sensory audit.

Figure 6.2 (page 166) illustrates how a high school language arts teacher might conduct a sensory audit.

Sensory audits can be valuable tools to help educators identify potential sensory barriers in their teaching environments, a critical first step to increasing the accessibility of their teaching spaces for all students.

Sensory Audit	
Location: Room 110, Visual Arts and Music Classroom	
Walkthrough 1: Potential Visual Issues	• The room is lit with fluorescent lighting. • The classroom is decorated with lots of brightly colored posters. • Student artwork is on the walls and on display in the case in the back of the room.

Walkthrough 2: Potential Auditory Issues	• There is limited soundproofing, and the classes next door can be heard. • The volume of the public address system is set at the highest level and cannot be changed from the classroom. • The public address system has feedback and other squeaks.
Walkthrough 3: Potential Tactile Issues	• Musical instruments are visible (tempting to touch). • Art supplies are visible (tempting to touch). • The art supplies have different textures (for example, paste, papier-mâché, clay, finger paint), which may cause issues for some students.
Walkthrough 4: Potential Olfactory Issues	• The classroom is located down the hall from the cafeteria. Students can smell food cooking as well as cleaning materials.
Walkthrough 5: Potential Gustatory Issues	• Nothing in the space should be eaten; however, some students may be tempted to eat paste and other art supplies. • The smell of food cooking in the cafeteria could bring about gustatory issues.

FIGURE 6.1: Conducting a comprehensive sensory audit of the learning environment—Elementary school visual arts and music classroom.

*Visit **go.SolutionTree.com/differentiatedinstruction** for a free reproducible version of this figure.*

Sensory Audit	
Location: Room 104, Language Arts Classroom	
Walkthrough 1: Potential Visual Issues	• The classroom has fluorescent lighting. • The classroom is decorated with posters. • The whiteboard is text heavy. • Poster paper with lists of words and terms can be found throughout the classroom.
Walkthrough 2: Potential Auditory Issues	• The classroom is located near the front of the building, and students can hear people in the lobby as they enter and exit. • The volume of the public address system is very low, is difficult to hear, and cannot be changed from the classroom.
Walkthrough 3: Potential Tactile Issues	• Books are out and visible (tempting to touch). • There are items on the teacher's desk that students might be tempted to touch.
Walkthrough 4: Potential Olfactory Issues	• On Monday mornings, after the floor of the classroom has been washed over the weekend, the classroom smells like detergent.
Walkthrough 5: Potential Gustatory Issues	• No potential gustatory issues were identified.

FIGURE 6.2: Conducting a comprehensive sensory audit of the learning environment—High school language arts classroom.

Addressing and Modulating the Identified Potential Sensory Issues in the Learning Environment

After identifying potential sources of sensory issues in the environment, the next step is for educators to determine some ways to alleviate those issues without adversely affecting student learning. Continuing from the previous example, figure 6.3 (page 168) shows one vehicle to help teachers analyze potential sensory issues and determine ways to address and modulate them.

With careful inventorying and planning, we can make our teaching more accessible before it begins by attending to sensory issues that might arise in our physical spaces. Next, we can turn to identifying and alleviating potential sensory issues in teaching and learning, both by modifying our lesson plans and by engaging strategies that help us respond to sensory issues in the moment.

In the Artist's Words

I like things that are soft and comfy. I want to create spaces where people can come in and feel disarmed because I think that's what textiles do really well, especially the fabrics that I use, which are colorful and playful and create connections of nostalgia to childhood. The audience then feels slightly vulnerable and disarmed. You're not coming at them with an aggressive message that you need to change, everything you are doing is wrong, and you're being ableist. It's more, you're entering this space, and you feel comfortable and playful. It's almost like returning to that experience of childhood where we can be open and honest. I think there's a vulnerability that comes with playing with textiles because they hold our collective memories. I'm drawn to them for so many reasons. And the softness—I think being soft is quite radical because we're always taught to be assertive and hard—everything from architecture to our technology. Our whole world is built this way. But when you come into a space that is colorful, bright, and filled with softness, and that is the primary experience of that space—again, it's pretty disarming. And people either love it or hate it. (A. C. Mills, personal communication, September 25, 2024)

—**Amy Claire Mills**, textile artist, curator, and producer

Sense	Source of Potential Issue	Ways to Address the Issue
Visual	• Fluorescent lighting	• Use lamps instead of overhead fluorescent lights. • Apply colored acetate gels over fluorescent light sources.
Visual	• Bulletin boards and walls filled with bright colors • Walls covered with poster paper with text	• Cover bulletin boards and wall displays with large tarps. • Decrease the density of bulletin board displays. • Designate several spans of wall space for no decorations.
Auditory	• Public address system volume and quality issues	• Install volume controls for the public address system in the classroom. • Upgrade the public address system.
Auditory	• Lack of soundproofing and the location of the classroom leading to distracting sounds outside	• Install soundproofing panels on classroom walls. • Add signage outside the classroom that states that class is in progress and requests that passersby be quiet.
Tactile	• Items that are tempting to touch	• Cover tempting items with tarps or sheets.
Tactile	• Specific art supplies	• Provide students with the option of wearing rubber gloves when dealing with materials of various textures.
Olfactory	• Smells in the classroom from the nearby cafeteria and the detergent from floor washing	• Encourage the use of baking soda–based cleaning products that absorb odors and scents.

Gustatory	• Temptation to eat paste and other art supplies	• Store tempting supplies in sealed containers that are away from students' view. • Provide students with only the amount of tempting materials they will use. • Post signage around the classroom about the proper use of art supplies.

FIGURE 6.3: Addressing and modulating potential sensory issues in the learning environment.

*Visit **go.SolutionTree.com/differentiatedinstruction** for a free reproducible version of this figure.*

Addressing Sensory Issues in Planned Learning Activities

Sensory issues may also be at play in the activities that we plan for our classes, rehearsals, and lessons. A careful analysis of our planned learning activities through the lens of the five external senses and the two internal senses can help reveal instances where students may experience sensory issues. Once educators have identified potential sensory issues, they can determine ways to reduce or remove them so they are less likely to come up during teaching and learning sessions.

Analyzing, revealing, and addressing sensory issues in planned activities might look something like the following.

- **Teacher-curated solution:** A high school social studies teacher intends to show a film in class about the civil rights movement. The film includes some footage that was shot in a shaky camera style, where the images shift and move unpredictably. Some students might experience sensory challenges watching footage in this style. Based on this analysis, the teacher decides against showing the entire film and instead selects excerpts to show, making sure the excerpts do not include any shaky camera footage.

- **Student-choice solution:** A dance teacher in a community arts program has created a new dance sequence. The choreography includes several instances where the dancers are required to move in one direction and then reverse their direction very quickly. These movements might present challenges to students with vestibular sensory issues, who may become dizzy or disoriented or lose their balance. To alleviate these potential sensory issues, the teacher creates an alternative choreography that does not include the quick directional shifts, and students have the opportunity to choose which dance sequence they would prefer to learn.
- **Adaptive-tool solution:** The fifth graders are working with their physical education teacher on relay races. Each team begins with a runner holding a wooden baton and completing their leg of the relay. When the runner reaches the next member of their team, they pass the baton to them, and the new runner takes over the race. Some students might experience tactile issues holding the baton because of its texture. To address this potential issue, the teacher provides the students with the option of wearing gloves during the relay activity.
- **Technological solution:** Students in middle school are taking an essay test about the book that they read in their English language arts class. Each student is using a pencil to write their answers to the questions in their notebook. Some students might experience proprioceptive issues having to do with the amount of physical pressure to use in their hand as they put pencil to paper. To address this potential issue, the teacher provides the students with the option of using a word processing program on a computer to respond to the test questions.

Continuing with the previous examples, figure 6.4 shows how teachers might analyze potential sensory issues in their learning activities and determine ways to address them.

Learning Activity	Potential Sensory Issue (Sense Involved)	Ways to Address the Issue	Type of Solution (Teacher Curated, Student Choice, Adaptive, or Technological)
Film about the civil rights movement	Shaky camera footage (visual)	Identify and show excerpts of the film that do not include shaky footage. Use a different film in class.	Teacher curated
Dance sequence	Quick reversals of direction (vestibular)	Create an alternative choreography. Slow down the reversals of direction in the original sequence.	Student choice
Relay race	Texture of baton (tactile)	Allow students to wear gloves during the relay-race activity if they wish to. Allow the student groups to choose which baton to use. Give them a range of options with different shapes and textures.	Adaptive
Essay test	Hand pressure with pencil and paper (proprioceptive)	Allow the students to use a word processing program on a computer if they wish to.	Technological

FIGURE 6.4: Addressing sensory issues in planned learning activities.

*Visit **go.SolutionTree.com/differentiatedinstruction** for a free reproducible version of this figure.*

Thus far, I have discussed some ways educators can engage in proactive identification, analysis, and planning to make their teaching more accessible for students who experience sensory issues. Sensory issues can also arise for students in the moment as teaching and learning are taking place. The following strategies can help educators address sensory issues as they come up in their day-to-day work with students.

Establishing Routines and Procedures for Sensory Issues

Educators can establish routines and procedures for sensory issues that might arise as part of their everyday work with their students. Learners feel that their potential needs are seen, heard, and validated when they know that their teacher is aware of sensory issues, is open to striving to alleviate them, and is prepared with tools and plans to do so.

COMMUNICATE ABOUT SENSORY ISSUES

First, and most importantly, students need an easy, effective, and safe way to communicate with their teacher when they encounter a sensory challenge—without drawing attention to themselves, without being required to state their needs publicly, and without being singled out in front of their classmates. To that end, teachers can provide their students with a nonverbal hand signal to use or a card to hold up if they are experiencing a sensory issue of some kind. This communication helps the teacher become aware of the situation and take steps to address the sensory issue at hand. If necessary, the teacher can quietly pull the student aside and ask a couple of clarifying questions to determine where the issue lies and what they can do to help.

Let's look at an example of how a student might use a nonverbal signal for a sensory issue. Eighth graders are listening to portions of a recording of Igor Stravinsky's *Rite of Spring* as part of a unit on early 20th century music in their music appreciation class. One excerpt features the entire orchestra playing quick, sharp, rhythmic accents in loud chords. When that segment begins, a student raises his hand with his fingers in an *O* shape—the class signal that is used for sensory issues. His teacher hands him a set of noise canceling headphones, and the student wears them for the remainder of the listening activity.

Even the most thoughtful analysis and planning on the teacher's part cannot fully eliminate possible sensory challenges for some students when it comes to interacting with media of various kinds. In certain cases, as in the previous example, music at a loud volume or with dense, thick instrumentation can lead to sensory issues. Sensory challenges can arise with other aspects of music, as well, such as its *range* (the highness or lowness of the pitches being played) and *timbre* (the qualities of the actual sounds of particular instruments or voices). Regarding the former, some individuals experience sensory issues with high-pitched or low-pitched sounds. In addition, for some people, sensory issues are connected with the qualities of certain types of sounds, such as the sound of the bassoon, the sound of the recorder, or the sound of bagpipes, to name a few of many possibilities.

Noise canceling headphones are a cost-effective tool that can help individuals who are sensitive to sounds manage their exposure to auditory stimuli. As in the preceding example, students can use noise canceling headphones when they are exposed to sounds that are loud, have dense instrumentation (many instruments playing at once), or have a particular quality that is challenging for them. Because they help focus auditory sensory input, noise canceling headphones can also be used to assist students who are easily distracted by background noise and ambient sounds. In these instances, students would use noise canceling headphones to effectively mute the sounds in the background, making it easier for them to pay attention, participate, and learn.

ASSEMBLE AND MAINTAIN A SENSORY TOOL KIT

Noise canceling headphones are just one of an array of materials educators can use to help address sensory challenges during their day-to-day activities with students. I strongly suggest teachers develop and maintain a *sensory tool kit*—a collection of items that they and their students can use on those occasions when sensory issues arise. The contents of the sensory tool kit could include the following.

- **Noise canceling headphones**
    + To decrease auditory stimulation by muting loud sounds or sounds with challenging timbres
    + To focus auditory input by muting background noise
- **Weighted pads**
    + To increase tactile stimulation
    + To provide soothing pressure
- **Noiseless fidget toys**
    + To increase tactile stimulation
    + To provide tactile input and movement opportunities for sensory-seeking students
    + To provide movement opportunities to soothe students
- **Sunglasses**
    + To decrease visual stimulation, particularly of bright lights or bright colors
- **Visors**
    + To decrease visual stimulation, particularly of overhead lights or visuals
    + To provide sensory stimulation on the head
- **Scarves**
    + To decrease tactile stimulation
    + To assist students with holding hands, whereby students hold one end of the scarf instead of holding hands
- **Gloves**
    + To decrease tactile stimulation
    + To support students with handling textured items
    + To assist students with holding hands

The previous example illustrates one instance of a teacher and a student using noise canceling headphones, part of the sensory tool kit. Consider a few more examples.

- A high school science class is hosting its annual science fair in the school cafeteria. The cafeteria is lit with fluorescent lighting. One of the students asks his teacher if he can bring a visor from the classroom to wear in the cafeteria. Wearing the visor, the student is able to participate in and learn effectively at the science fair.
- At the beginning of the drama class at the community arts center, the twelve-year-old students sit in a circle with their teacher for their opening sharing session. One of the students is having a difficult time quieting their body—they are moving and shifting and appear to be unable to sit in one place. The teacher brings the student a weighted pad and puts it on their shoulders. After a few moments, the student is able to settle down and participate in the sharing session along with their classmates.
- A mathematics teacher is standing at the whiteboard, explaining long division to her class of third graders. One of the students is having a difficult time concentrating on what the teacher is saying and is patting her hands on her desk. The teacher hands the student a stress ball. As the student squeezes the stress ball, she is better able to focus and pay attention in class.

DEVELOP PROCEDURES FOR WHOLE-CLASS SENSORY BREAKS

One very effective way to increase the accessibility of your teaching from a sensory perspective is through whole-class sensory breaks. Whole-class sensory breaks are opportunities for all students to step away from the learning activity and recalibrate their senses through movement, such as through stretching, ball passing, jumping jacks and other calisthenics, parachute games, dancing, yoga poses, and more. The teacher or a designated student can lead the movement activities, with students taking turns leading different activities. On some occasions, whole-class sensory breaks can coincide with transitions and can be as short as one or two minutes in duration. At other times, a whole-class sensory break might last for five or ten minutes. When it comes to whole-class sensory breaks, teachers can determine the timing and duration that are the best match for the flow of their classes and for their particular groups of students.

CREATE PROCEDURES AND A SPACE FOR INDIVIDUAL SENSORY BREAKS

When sensory challenges arise for particular students, educators can provide support through an individual sensory break. *Individual sensory breaks* are bounded periods of time spent in a quiet space with as little sensory stimulation as possible. Individual sensory breaks can be particularly effective for students who feel overwhelmed by their sensory issues, either because their senses are extremely overstimulated or understimulated. In these instances, the most effective course of action for supporting the student may be for them to remove themselves from the stimuli altogether.

Individual sensory breaks work best when teachers have developed, established, and communicated clear and consistent procedures for them. These procedures should include the following elements.

- **The manner in which students request an individual sensory break:** Students should understand exactly what to do to request an individual sensory break. Ideally, they would make these requests through a form of nonverbal communication (such as by making a hand signal or holding up a card) so they are not singled out in front of their peers.
- **The number of students you will allow to take an individual sensory break at the same time:** There should be a stated policy regarding the number of students who may take an individual sensory break at one time. I suggest this number be quite small (one or two at most).

Keeping the number of students who are permitted to take a sensory break at either one or two helps ensure that individual sensory breaks are manageable for the teacher. It also can guard against the potential slippery slope of many students requesting individual sensory breaks; however, if multiple students are requesting sensory breaks at the same time, the teacher should seriously consider implementing a whole-class sensory break.

- **The length of individual sensory breaks:** Individual sensory breaks should last no more than five minutes. Students should use a timer to ensure they complete their sensory break and rejoin the class after five minutes.
- **The location of individual sensory breaks:** Many educators who have their own classrooms create a sensory-break corner for this purpose. A sensory-break corner is a designated area located away from the main body of the classroom but in a place where the teacher can see the student. The space usually features soft lighting and often includes sensory support materials, such as large pillows or bean bag furniture, noise canceling headphones, fidget toys, and weighted pads. A sensory break can also take the form of students leaving the space (briefly) altogether, such as by going to the water fountain, going to the bathroom, or assisting the teacher by bringing papers to the office or to another classroom, for a few examples.

Sensory issues can present significant barriers to student engagement, participation, and learning. Educators can start with sensory accessibility when it comes to their teaching environments and planned activities through careful inventorying, analysis, preparation, and adjustments. If sensory issues occur during the course of lessons and activities, sensory breaks (both for the whole class and for individuals), sensory-break corners, and a tool kit of materials can provide students with the sensory support, calming, or stimulation they need to learn effectively.

Takeaways

Not long after the smoke detector incident that I relayed at the beginning of this chapter, I attended a three-day yoga and meditation retreat in the Berkshires. While I was there, I was surprised to discover that another sense plays a more important role in my life than I had previously thought.

I discovered that I have a close and powerful relationship with my olfactory sense, and the scents around me can change me physically and energetically. When I arrived at the retreat center, I was immediately struck by the way the facility smelled and its effect on me. It engulfed me like a cozy blanket of relaxation, calming my energy. I could feel its impact on a biological level: My heart rate and my respiration began to slow down. My inner pacing started to shift and lessen in intensity. My movements calmed. My steps slowed. I took more time than usual to observe my surroundings. And this was *before* I had taken any yoga classes or participated in any meditation sessions! All it took to make these differences was for me to be in the proximity of that particular scent.

Later that first day, I went to the shop on site and asked the staff to help me replicate this sensory experience at home. Together, we determined that the scent I was looking for is a combination of eucalyptus and lavender. I purchased some room sprays, essential oils, and a diffuser so that I could bring the scent to my home and office, and I have been using them on a regular basis ever since.

We are all affected by our sensory input, and many of us experience sensory issues of some kind. As educators, we have the opportunity to create environments and facilitate activities for our students, many of whom may experience sensory issues. In some cases, these sensory issues can interfere with their engagement, participation, and learning, rendering the educational experience inaccessible to them.

This chapter aimed to help educators develop a deeper understanding of and appreciation for sensory challenges that their students may encounter. The strategies I discussed here can help teachers increase the accessibility of their teaching when it comes to sensory issues. By attending to the sensory stimuli in our teaching settings and learning activities, making adjustments when possible, and utilizing a range of tools in the moment, we can strive to reduce and remove sensory barriers and make it possible for more of our students to learn effectively.

In the Artist's Words

Particularly for autistic people, it's not necessarily the volume that's the issue. It's the sound itself that's the issue. This is why there are so many autistic people who adore death metal and other things like that. And so the problem is with a lot of venues, when they're trying to do accessible events, they then do really quiet, chill music. Which, I mean, it's lovely. . . . They just do a quiet music concert, which sounds really chill, to just be in the center of London and just go hide in the concert hall for an hour, listening to quiet music, it does sound ideal, but that's not the only way to be accessible. It's the enjoyment of the sound. And also the other thing, as well, is when you are making the sound it's a very different kind of experience to it. And so, yeah, the feeling and connection to it is different. (B. Lunn, personal communication, September 10, 2024)

—**Ben Lunn**, composer, conductor, and founder of the Disabled Artist Network

I like to specialize in teaching neurodivergent students. I teach quite a number of autistic children and adults, and some of them are extremely rewarding. And actually, the most rewarding student I've ever had was before I knew I was autistic, but I knew he was. And he's an amazing musician. He's actually much better than me. He came to me from the age of nine, for about ten years he came to me. And he couldn't read music because he had trouble with reading, but he just could remember everything. And so we did everything by ear, so I would play a bar and he'd copy me. And like that we'd learn really complicated pieces, and he could just remember them forever. And he went on to do a music degree and is now working as a musician.

—Madge Woollard, pianist and piano teacher

CHAPTER 7
BRING IT ALL TOGETHER

Every educator I know who has taught for at least a couple of years—regardless of the context, subject area, or students—has experienced some form of what I have dubbed *mandate fatigue*.

Mandate fatigue denotes the sense of exhaustion and disillusionment teachers feel in reaction to a seemingly endless parade of new required systems, procedures, or approaches that are thrust on them by well-meaning administrators. Having endured various manifestations of mandates—such as new curriculum sequences, documentation procedures, training sessions, and assessment requirements—educators, to put it plainly, are tired. They are tired of all the effort it takes to remake, redo, reframe, and relearn. They are also tired of hearing promises that some new system, procedure, program, philosophy, approach, or strategy will transform their practice, revolutionize their school, and solve every issue or challenge they have ever faced or will ever encounter.

I am very well acquainted with mandate fatigue. I have lost count of the number of new requirements of various kinds that have been imposed on me throughout my career as an educator. I am still on the receiving end of them today. I pride myself on being an optimistic, "glass half full" person who embraces the generative opportunities that accompany change. However, I must confess: When it comes to these sorts of directives, because of my history with mandates, my first reaction is a weary and cynical "Here we go again." I simply can no longer muster enthusiasm, hope, or excited anticipation. My mandate fatigue is showing by preventing me from being open to new ideas.

The last thing I want to do is contribute to anyone's mandate fatigue. That was never the intention of this book, and that is not accessible arts education. This book is not a mandate—it is an invitation. It invites you to incorporate the principles, habits of mind, and strategies of accessible arts education into your teaching practice in the ways that are most relevant and meaningful for you, your teaching context, and your students.

Accessible arts education is not a mandate; rather, it is an approach that can help you reduce and remove barriers that may be obstructing student engagement, participation, and learning, thereby making the educational enterprise that you facilitate more accessible for all learners.

When you read a book like this one, it is common to experience a range of reactions—perhaps one at a time, or maybe even all at once. You might feel excited about what you've encountered, intrigued to learn more, motivated to experiment, skeptical about what could be possible in your setting due to logistic or structural constraints, and more. All of these are intertwined with what I suspect you are wondering in some way: "What do I do now?"

The following sections support you as you prepare to incorporate aspects of accessible arts education into your teaching practice. First, I share some advice for you to consider as you get started, as well as some thoughts for you to keep in mind along the way. Then, I explore several real-world applications of accessible arts education principles and pedagogy. I conclude by discussing the implications of accessible arts education for individual educators and for the field of education at large.

Advice for Educators

Now that we've established what accessible arts education is (a framework of principles, habits of mind, and strategies) and is not (a mandate), I continue to use this frame for the following advice to support you as you prepare to implement accessible arts education into your practice.

- **Pick and choose:** Accessible arts education is not a new, soup-to-nuts pedagogical system that must be adopted wholesale. I encourage you to choose and try aspects of accessible arts education that make the most sense for your particular teaching situation and for your particular students. There will be certain elements of accessible arts education that will be more relevant, meaningful, and effective for your teaching, and you should focus on those and not bother with the others. Pick and choose the pieces of accessible arts education that resonate most with your teaching, your context, and your students, and implement those.
- **Celebrate uniqueness:** Accessible arts education is not one-size-fits-all. It is not a recipe. Accessible arts education, by its very nature, takes on different forms in different settings, and even on different days in the same setting. Simply put, accessible arts education looks different everywhere and every time it happens. And it should; the enterprise of making educational experiences more accessible must be tailored and customized to be effective. While they may unfold uniquely, all expressions of accessible arts education share two key aims: (1) to reduce and remove barriers to student engagement, participation, and learning and (2) to increase opportunities for people to learn and grow.
- **Celebrate, expect, and relish the uniqueness of how accessible arts education takes shape in your teaching:** There is no "correct" way to implement accessible arts education. If you are incorporating any accessible arts education principles, habits of mind, or strategies as a means of striving to increase access to the educational experiences that you provide for your students, then you are engaging in accessible arts education.

- **Approach the process with flexibility:** Accessible arts education is not static. It is not "set it and forget it." It can—and should—change and morph in the moment in response to what has just happened or in anticipation of what needs to happen next. Furthermore, an accessible arts education strategy that was useful and valuable one day may not be helpful another day, even in the same situation or with the same students. Teaching and learning are complex, dynamic endeavors and processes, and accessible arts education must be responsive to all of that complexity to be effective. Approach your use of accessible arts education strategies with flexibility and be prepared to tweak and adapt as you go. Embrace the dynamic nature of accessible arts education and the opportunities that it opens up for you to improvise and create as an educator.
- **Incorporate slowly:** Accessible arts education does not necessitate that you jettison your current pedagogy and replace it with something entirely different. On the contrary, its habits of mind and key questions (discussed in chapter 1, page 26) provide a framework for thinking differently about the wonderful work that you already do as an educator, and its strategies and tools guide and assist you as you strive to make your teaching more effective for every student you meet. Incorporate accessible arts education into your teaching practice slowly and methodically, one piece at a time. I suggest that you think about the process as follows.
    a. Begin with one thing (one strategy, one tool, one barrier to accessibility, one aspect of accessible arts education) that will be easy to incorporate into your existing teaching practice with little to no extra work.
    b. Try that one thing and see how it goes. Give it a bit of time (multiple implementations, more than one class meeting). You may not observe its effect right away; some of the tools of accessible arts education take time to yield visible results.

c. Continue with that one thing for a while. See if you start to notice its impact on particular students or on groups of students. How is the thing that you've tried making a difference in the accessibility of your teaching?

d. You might choose to stop here and just stay with that one thing. By all means, do so if it feels right for you and if it opens up access in the ways you need it to for your students. That one thing may be sufficient—for now, or for a long time.

e. Try one more thing only when you are ready and the need arises. If you become aware of an issue with accessibility that you can address through additional avenues and are ready to do so, try one more thing and watch how it goes. As with the first thing you tried, give the new thing a bit of time. It might take a while before the aspect of accessible arts education that you've added makes a discernible difference for your student(s).

f. Stop trying things whenever you need to stop doing so, for any reason.

g. Try more things when you are ready to do so and when you have identified challenges with accessibility that you would like to lessen for your student(s).

- **Release yourself from unrealistic expectations:** Accessible arts education does not require you to possess deep knowledge and understanding of how every student learns best. Returning to the discussion in chapter 1 (page 17), accessible arts education principles, habits of mind, strategies, tools, and tweaks improve every educator's teaching by reducing and removing barriers to engagement, participation, and learning that every learner may encounter. As principle 1 states (page 25), they are necessary for some students and helpful for all.

  A number of educators have shared with me that they feel as though they have failed at their jobs because they are not well versed in the specific ways that each of their students learns best. Some have even told me they are ashamed that a whole week or month or semester has gone by, and they are not yet experts in how all their students learn. These teachers are beating themselves up because they have placed an expectation on themselves that they can never reach.

To these educators, and to you, I advise the following: Getting to know your students and how they learn takes a lot of time. You are neither expected nor required to be well versed in the learning of every one of your students. Frankly, it is not humanly possible for most of us. Think of community educators who may see their students only once per week for an hour-long meeting, or collegiate faculty who teach large lecture courses, or middle and high school teachers who teach multiple sections of an array of classes, or arts educators who might work with several hundred (or more) students per week, for just a few examples. Furthermore, it is an unreasonable and unfair expectation. We are dedicated to and passionate about our students' learning, and we desire to be the very best educators we can be. And while there is nothing wrong—on the contrary, there is everything right—about that dedication, passion, and desire, we need to ensure they do not translate to our holding ourselves to unattainable standards.

Being curious about, noticing, observing, and asking how your students learn are useful, productive, and commendable approaches to teaching, learning, and accessibility. Because you are deeply invested in nurturing your students' growth and development, you will be curious about how your students learn, and you will strive to understand it to the best of your ability over time. But it's important that you set realistic expectations for yourself. When it comes to how your students learn best, you will gain the insights you can gain, and you won't gain the insights that you cannot gain (for whatever reason). As all of this plays out over time, no matter how it proceeds for you, there is absolutely nothing to feel ashamed about and absolutely no instance whatsoever of any failure on your part. Release yourself from the expectation that you must be an expert in how all your students learn best to be able to attend to issues of accessibility. Remember that deep knowledge of your students' learning is not a requirement or a prerequisite for implementing accessible arts education tools and strategies.

- **Embrace the lack of predictability:** Accessible arts education tools and strategies are not guaranteed to increase accessibility every time you employ them. The educational enterprise, with its many elements, dynamics, relationships, and processes, is extremely—and fascinatingly—complex. As we know all too well, teaching and learning do not take place in sterile laboratories where variables can be isolated; rather, they are human endeavors that are delightfully messy and can be influenced in many ways by an infinite number of factors (some that we can think of or point to and some that we cannot). In actual practice, a tool or strategy that is effective at increasing access and diminishing boundaries for a student or a group of students one day may not be nearly as effective with the same student(s) in the same situation the next day. This is no different from any aspect of pedagogy. Just as there are no guarantees that any aspect of pedagogy will be successful all the time, the same is true of accessible arts education. A tool or approach that addresses issues of access in one situation may not do so again, even under seemingly identical circumstances. Revel in the success of the strategies when they are effective and be prepared to tweak them or try something else when they are not.
- **Create your own tools:** The pedagogy of accessible arts education is not limited to the contents of this book. Absolutely not! In fact, one of the most stimulating and

vibrant aspects of accessible arts education is that it is a generative approach that continues to grow every day in new and astonishing ways. As they engage in their teaching practice, educators create and discover new avenues to facilitate accessibility, which leads them to develop new teaching tools of various kinds that advance accessibility for their students. With the principles and habits of mind of accessible arts education as guideposts, there truly is no limit to accessible arts education pedagogy. Use the principles and habits of mind to guide you as you attempt and explore outside-the-box ideas to discover your own ways to lessen barriers that might be impeding your students' access to engagement, participation, and learning.

In the Artist's Words

One of the first and most important musical things I learned was how to improvise. Playing by ear was already natural for me, since I would replicate what I heard on the radio, but I really had to develop that skill since I can't sight-read and play my instrument simultaneously. Eventually, this became pattern recognition. These chords at the end of a bridge usually mean a song will get quieter and drums will drop out. These chords in that beautiful stripped-down chorus mean we're probably going to build back up into a chorus with full dynamics! There's so much nuance in the instruments around me that even if I've never rehearsed a song, I can probably create a part that will fit in because I've spent so much time studying how to listen. To this day, I still practice by turning on the radio and spinning the dial. I play to whatever comes on, and all the better if that's a song I've never heard before. It builds my repertoire, but it also reminds me to listen. (Perez, 2022)

—**Shane Lowe**, percussionist and music director

Accessible Arts Education in Practice

The following vignettes provide real-world examples of ways that teachers can use accessible arts education and tools to reduce and remove barriers to student engagement, participation, and learning. Four common barriers provide the frame through which these brief stories of practice are shared. While they are situated in particular educational contexts, their strategies and tools can easily be adapted broadly and implemented in any subject area, in any setting, and with any students.

Barrier 1: Many Levels in the Same Class

One of the most common questions I hear from educators has to do with the challenges of teaching a class where the students vary greatly in terms of their level of skill or knowledge. The following example illustrates some ways teachers can address these challenges and make it possible for all students, regardless of their level, to learn and grow. While the following example features a high school chorus, teachers can apply these accessible arts education strategies to any educational setting.

The freshman chorus includes students at vastly different levels of skill, knowledge, and experience in music. Some are highly skilled at reading music, while others have learned all their pieces by rote. Some have developed strong posture, breathing, and voice placement skills, while others have never studied vocal technique. Some can pronounce Italian lyrics correctly, while others have sung only in English. These differences among the students act as a barrier to every student's engagement, participation, and learning in freshman chorus. They also present unique challenges to their choral director, who is the only teacher for the entire ensemble.

To reduce and remove this barrier, the choral director employs the following accessible arts education strategies.

- **Peer teaching:** Students are assigned to work in groups where the more experienced and more knowledgeable classmates will teach their colleagues. First, the choral director provides the groups with materials (such as music reading exercises and assignments to complete, vocal technique elements to practice together, and song lyrics in other languages to learn). The groups work on their own, with specific roles and responsibilities assigned to each member of the group, and the choral director visits each group to answer questions and check on their work together.

- **Differentiated independent work:** The choral director begins the rehearsal by outlining the topic of the day. Next, she hands out packets for independent work. She created three different sets of packets based on level of difficulty: a packet of introductory and early-stage materials for beginner students, a packet of intermediate materials for students at that level, and a packet of advanced materials for students who are ready for additional challenges. The teacher gives each chorister the packet that corresponds to their level of skill, knowledge, and experience with the day's topic. The freshmen complete the tasks in the handout packets on their own, starting at the beginning of the packet and progressing through it in order. The choral director walks around the classroom and checks in with each student to answer questions and sign off on tasks that students have completed correctly. At the end of class, the choral director brings the students together for a brief discussion about what they learned about the day's topic from their various assignments.
- **Student choice:** After introducing the subject of their work for this activity, the choral director provides the choristers with the opportunity to choose from four stations with assignments and tasks related to the subject at hand. For example, if the students are to work on their Italian pronunciation skills, the stations might include:
    + Recordings of native Italian speakers saying the words of song lyrics that students listen to before recording themselves saying the same words

+ International Phonetic Alphabet cards that students use as a reference to help them write out lyrics using the International Phonetic Alphabet
+ A list of rules for correct Italian pronunciation, along with Italian words for students to practice saying according to those rules
+ Recordings of people speaking Italian words incorrectly, to which students listen to identify the errors and write down how to correct them

The students select a station, go to that part of the classroom, and complete the tasks and assignments at their station. When they have completed their activities, the students share their work with their classmates, and the choral director leads a discussion about what the students learned.

Barrier 2: Repeated Disruptions From One Student

Educators often ask what to do when one student repeatedly disrupts the class. The disruptive student behavior could take a range of forms, such as:

- Not following instructions
- Walking around the room when everyone else is seated
- Hitting other students or calling people names
- Speaking or making noise during class

I remind teachers that student behavior usually stems from an underlying cause. It provides a clue that something else is going on for the individual: They may be easily distracted, they might encounter difficulties with sitting or being still for long periods of time, they may be hungry, they may be tired, or they may feel anxious or otherwise unsafe in the classroom. Sometimes, the underlying cause can be quite simple for teachers to detect and address. At other times, it can be helpful to seek additional information by checking in with other colleagues who teach the same student or by speaking with the student privately.

Identifying the underlying cause of the disruptive behavior can open pathways to address that behavior. For example, a student who is not following instructions because they are easily distracted might benefit from visual representations of instructions or a new seat assignment. A learner who encounters difficulties sitting or being still for long periods of time might benefit from movement breaks or an altered flow of class activities to lessen the amount of time spent seated or still. A student who hits other people because they do not feel safe in the classroom might benefit from additional classroom routines or mindfulness activities, such as short meditations.

The following story features one particular form of disruptive student behavior: a fixation on a particular topic. The strategies I discuss here easily transfer to other kinds of repeated student disruption, as well.

Alexander, a fourth grader, is extremely passionate about dinosaurs. He loves to read about them and think about them. He spends all his spare time learning about dinosaurs: on the internet, at exhibits, through documentaries, and more. When it comes to dinosaurs, Alexander knows many, many facts and has mastered lots of information, and he feels compelled to tell everything he can to everyone he meets. Alexander's intense, singular focus on dinosaurs acts as a barrier to his engagement, participation, and learning in school. All Alexander ever wants to think about or talk about is dinosaurs. As a result, his academic work is suffering. His classmates experience this barrier, as well. Alexander makes unrelated comments about dinosaurs again and again during his classes, disrupting the lessons and interfering with everyone's learning.

To reduce this barrier, Alexander's teachers collaborated on implementing a consistent set of accessible arts education strategies in all their classrooms.

- **New procedures:** Speak with Alexander privately before class begins. Explain that you know he loves dinosaurs and really wants to share what he knows about dinosaurs with you. Tell him that you would really like to hear what he has to say about dinosaurs and will set a special time with him to do so.

- **Structured boundaries:** Arrange with Alexander that he can talk with you about dinosaurs for five minutes every day before class begins. But once class begins, he must stop talking about dinosaurs and participate in the class activities along with the other students.
- **Clear sequences:** Use a First-Then summary statement to summarize the procedure.

"First, you and I will talk for five minutes about dinosaurs; then it will be time for class. No dinosaurs during class."

- **Written contract:** Write the First-Then summary statement on a piece of paper that you and Alexander sign as your agreement about when he can talk about dinosaurs.
- **Consistent implementation:** Follow the new procedure at every class meeting. Spend the five minutes before class with Alexander for a conversation about dinosaurs. Keep the amount of time to five minutes and restate the First-Then summary statement to remind him of your agreement. Every time Alexander tries to interrupt class with a comment about dinosaurs, give him a gentle but firm reminder that there is to be no talk of dinosaurs during class. It may take some time for Alexander to grow accustomed to the new procedure. Consistent implementation by all the teachers who work with Alexander will help him come to understand what is expected of him at school and will eventually address the issue.

Three additional sets of strategies that can be effective with disruptive students are outlined in the following scenes. In all of these cases, teachers create opportunities for the students to shine and distinguish themselves positively, based on what they know, on what they can do, and on how they can be helpful.

1. **Opportunities for connections:** When it can contribute to learning in a meaningful way, make connections to dinosaurs in class as a way to honor Alexander's expertise and recruit his interest and engagement. A few examples include:
   + For a poetry assignment, encourage Alexander to write a poem about dinosaurs.
   + For a research paper assignment about animals and their habitats, Alexander could write a paper about dinosaurs and their habitats.
   + For a mathematics assignment, Alexander might use a scenario about dinosaurs as the basis for writing a word problem for his classmates to solve.
   + For an assignment where students read a book of their choice, provide Alexander with a reading-level-appropriate book about dinosaurs.
   + For a dance assignment, Alexander could use the movements of different dinosaurs to demonstrate weight and pacing in choreography.

2. **Student expertise:** When appropriate, provide Alexander with opportunities to take on the role of dinosaur expert in class. Some examples include:
   + Create a culture of recognizing and valuing student expertise in the classroom. Ask each student to share something they feel they are good at or know a great deal about. Students can use statements like "I am a really good skateboarder," "I know a lot about gardening," or "I am a dinosaur expert."
   + When a student's area of expertise comes up, consult the student expert and encourage them to help, teach, or share what they know in a way that contributes to the class and to the lesson or activity.
   + If it is connected with class topics and activities, ask Alexander to share something that he knows about dinosaurs. Lay out clear parameters and make sure that

he sticks to them so that Alexander understands how much you would like him to share and when you will need him to stop sharing. Sample parameters include:

"Tell us your three favorite dinosaur facts."

"Tell us one thing you know about dinosaurs that relates to this lesson."

"You have five minutes—tell us some important facts about the triceratops."

The previous examples and strategies have centered on the disruptive behavior that occurs when a student is fixated on a particular topic. While these strategies can certainly be effective in those instances when the disruptive student engages in other forms of behavior (such as talking out, interrupting the teacher, or raising their hand again and again), let's take a moment to discuss one additional strategy better suited to those other behaviors. Sometimes, these sorts of disruptions occur because the student is seeking attention from the teacher or because they wish to develop a closer relationship with the teacher. This strategy can often transform what had been negative, disruptive behavior into positive attention and relationships.

3. **Student assistant:** Create a unique and prestigious job for the disruptive student in your classroom. Providing the conditions for the student to make positive contributions to the class and to be singled out based on what they can do well encourages constructive, helpful behavior and often extinguishes the disruptive behavior. For example, the student could:
   + Provide administrative help by taking attendance, handing out materials, or collecting assignments
   + Write key words on the board
   + Set up furniture or materials
   + Clean up the classroom

Barrier 3: The Assignment, Project, or Task Itself

Sometimes, the barrier to student engagement, participation, or learning lies in the assignment, project, or task itself. In these instances, a simple reframing may be all that is necessary to increase accessibility.

Students in a middle school science class are required to memorize a list of ten common chemical formulas for an upcoming test. The teacher gives the list of formulas to the students and explains that they will need to memorize the formulas for an exam in two weeks. When it comes time for the exam, Michelle is unable to remember any of the formulas. She leaves her test paper blank, and her grade on the exam is zero. When her teacher asks her what happened, Michelle confesses that she did not memorize the formulas.

In this case, the barrier to Michelle's learning is located in the assignment itself. Specifically, when she looked at the list of formulas, she was overwhelmed by the amount of information she was required to memorize. Ten formulas was too much material for her to take in all at once. She didn't know where to begin with the memorization assignment, so she didn't do the assignment at all.

I have seen this issue come up for a number of individuals over the years. Many people, because of the ways their brains process visual stimuli, can become overwhelmed when they are asked to take in, learn, or memorize a large amount of text or information.

One accessible arts education strategy that can lessen this barrier is to provide the information or materials in smaller chunks rather than all at once. Rather than giving the students a handout with all ten formulas, the teacher could provide fewer formulas at a time and add new formulas gradually. The teacher could provide the formulas on a schedule like the following.

- **Week 1**
    a. *Monday*—Students receive two formulas they must memorize by Wednesday.
    b. *Wednesday*—Students receive three additional formulas they must memorize by Friday.
    c. *Friday*—Students take a quiz on the first five formulas.

- **Week 2**
    a. *Monday*—The teacher reviews the first five formulas in class. Students receive two additional formulas they must memorize by Wednesday.
    b. *Wednesday*—Students receive three additional formulas they must memorize by Friday.
    c. *Friday*—Students take the exam on all ten formulas.

By assigning the formulas in smaller pieces with less material to memorize at once, the teacher reduces the barrier that had been in the larger assignment. This simple tweak to the framing of the memorization task makes it more accessible to all students.

Generally speaking, when students engage with smaller chunks—amounts of information provided at once, steps in a task analysis, and numbers of words in verbal instructions, for just a few examples—the experience is more accessible for more learners. Larger pieces, amounts, steps, and numbers of items can sometimes be too large, and therefore serve as barriers for some learners.

Barrier 4: The Removal of Supports

Teachers often provide supports of various kinds to help students as they begin learning something new. A colleague once referred to this as "having the training wheels on." Once students can perform the task or execute the skill successfully with the supports in place, the teacher removes the supports, and the student attempts the task or skill unsupported. However, sometimes the very removal of supports can backfire, acting as a barrier to student learning rather than as a facilitator of student independence.

Let's look at an example. Adult students in a beginner piano class at a local community music school are learning how to play a new piece of music. Their teacher hands out copies of the sheet music and instructs the students to write in the letter names of each note in pencil, just below the notes. The teacher explains that the students will use their annotated sheet music for the next two weeks, and the written-in letter names will help them learn the piece. Two weeks later, the teacher collects the copies of the music the students used and replaces them with copies of the same piece of music, but without any written-in letter names. She then asks each student to play a section of the piece for the class using the new handout they just received.

The teacher is surprised that some of the students are not able to play the piece using the new sheet music handout with no annotations. After all, they had two weeks to practice the piece with the note names written on the music. Shouldn't they be able to perform it without the note names by now?

In this case, the barrier lies in the modulation of the supports—specifically, in the pace at which the teacher decreased the supports. The piano students went from being 100 percent supported, with letter names written in for all the notes on the page, to being 0 percent supported, with no written letter names at all. This transition was too large and too abrupt.

The accessible arts education strategy that can reduce this barrier is to modulate supports much more gradually and reduce them at a slower pace. In the case of the piano class, a sequence of steps like the one in the following list would be more effective.

1. The students write all the letter names for all the notes on the page and practice with their annotated sheet music for two weeks.
2. The students remove one annotation (one letter every time it appears) from their sheet music and practice with it for two weeks.
3. The students remove a second annotation (a different letter every time it appears) from their sheet music and practice with it for two weeks.
4. The students continue these steps until they can play the piece with sheet music that contains no annotations.

In this particular example, the piano teacher should choose the order of the removal of the letter names based on the key of the piece and should begin with the most common note, then turn to the second most common note, and so on. If the music is in the key of C, C is likely to be the first note name to remove, followed by G, followed by E, and so on.

The transition from fully supported to fully independent is too abrupt for many students. A more accessible approach is to decrease supports very gradually and at a slower pace. Put another way, going from 100 percent supported to 90 percent supported (rather than from 100 to 0) makes it possible for more students to participate in their learning journeys toward independence.

Takeaways

As you can see, rather than a mandate, this book is an invitation to:

- Take up the lens of anticipating, identifying, and seeking to reduce or remove barriers to student engagement and learning
- Think broadly and creatively about teaching, learning, student engagement, and assessment
- Find one simple way to incorporate any aspect of the principles, habits of mind, and strategies of accessible arts education into your practice
- Ground your approaches to making teaching and learning more accessible in your specific situation—for your students, in your setting, in your subject area, with your curriculum

From my perspective, this is where the true artistry of teaching comes into play. We create, plan, tweak, improvise, actualize, refine, and adjust through an ongoing, interactive process with our students. Education becomes an artistic process of creativity and exploration. When this process works well, teaching and learning take on an aesthetic quality—they actually become works of art. I have witnessed it again and again: As educators and their students cocreate accessible and effective teaching and learning opportunities together, something magical and artful happens.
As is so often the case when it comes to the arts, it is difficult, if not

impossible, to use words to describe it, but there is no mistaking it when it happens.

I invite you to experience this form of magical teaching artistry firsthand. The principles, habits of mind, and strategies shared in this book are just some of the tools you can use to make the magic happen with your students, in your setting, and in your subject area. All it takes is being open to possibility and willing to leap into a bit of uncertainty—just as artists approach their creative process.

In the Artist's Words

[My music teacher in school] was so nice. And for a guy like me, his response to my weirdness in music, my ADHD-ness, was to encourage it, and . . . enliven the flame, rather than dump me. I'd say, "I'm interested in the trumpet," and he would go, "Great! Here's an extra trumpet. . . . You don't know how to play notes? Let's look online." And so he would let me bounce around instruments all throughout middle school.

And he would tell this story for years after I graduated. It was something apparently hilarious to him that at one concert, a jazz concert, I was playing the electric bass. And there was a song, I hadn't told him, I think it was [the theme from] *Pink Panther*, and I stood up out of my chair and I put the bass in the chair upward. So it's an electric bass but I stood it up because I had told him for weeks and weeks that I wanted to play a stand-up bass, but I'm a very short person. And he was like, "My love, there is no, not even a ¾ bass. . . . You can't, you literally can't, you cannot reach up here."

And so I, grumpy, went away and schemed, and then on the day of the concert I took my electric bass and propped it up in the chair and played it. Like a vertical. And I did the whole *Pink Panther* [theme song]. And he's just, like, so shocked and excited. And he would tell that story forever that I turned the electric bass into a stand-up bass. (S. Tonti, personal communication, September 17, 2024)

—**Stephen Tonti**, ADHD coach and influencer, public speaker, and writer and producer for film and television

EPILOGUE

I began this book by writing about my lifelong dedication to making learning visible. For me, making learning visible means ensuring that learning is seen, celebrated, validated, and known. In the ensuing pages, I have elaborated on one powerful way to do just that: by increasing the accessibility of educational experiences for all students, no matter how they learn best.

Accessible arts education frames increasing accessibility in terms of anticipating, reducing, and striving to remove barriers that may obstruct student engagement, participation, and learning. The reasoning is simple: Fewer barriers permit greater access. And greater access to the educational enterprise facilitates visible learning for greater numbers of students. Therefore, the power of accessible arts education lies in the many ways that learning becomes visible when access becomes possible.

For me, writing this book is another important step in my lifelong quest to make learning visible. I wish to share the principles, habits of mind, and pedagogical strategies of accessible arts education with as many educators as possible so that, together, we can strive to make learning visible—and possible—for more people.

As you incorporate aspects of accessible arts education into your teaching practice, please get in touch with me on Instagram (@rhodabernard41) or LinkedIn (@rhoda-bernard-075a6710b). I want to hear about what accessible arts education means to you. I want to know how you will implement it in your teaching setting. I want to find out about the new strategies and tools you will create and use. What I want most of all is to learn from you and your students—and to ensure that, as we learn together, our learning is visible.

REFERENCES AND RESOURCES

ABA Educational Resources. (n.d.). *Social Stories*. Accessed at https://abaresources.com/social-stories on November 25, 2024.

Acevedo, B. (2025, May 9). What is sensory processing sensitivity? Traits, insights, and ADHD links. *ADDitude*. Accessed at www.additudemag.com/highly-sensitive-person-sensory-processing-sensitivity-adhd on September 14, 2024.

ADA Site Compliance. (2023, March 3). *Accessible fonts*. Accessed at https://adasitecompliance.com/accessible-fonts on June 1, 2024.

Akeret, J. (Director & Producer). (2002). *Someone sang for me: A portrait of educator Jane Sapp* [Film].

Alta Pediatrics. (n.d.). *Understanding sensory processing disorder*. Accessed at https://altapediatrics.com/resources/education-center/sensory-processing-disorder on September 14, 2024.

American Alliance for Theatre & Education. (n.d.). *Inclusive theatre*. Accessed at www.aate.com/inclusive-theatre-sig on April 7, 2025.

American Foundation for the Blind. (n.d.). *Tips and tricks to improve web accessibility*. Accessed at www.afb.org/consulting/afb-accessibility-resources/tips-and-tricks on June 1, 2024.

Americans With Disabilities Act of 1990, 42 U.S.C. § 12101 *et seq*. (1990).

Apple, M. W. (1979). *Ideology and curriculum*. Routledge.

Arendt, R. E., MacLean, W. E., Jr., & Baumeister, A. A. (1988). Critique of sensory integration therapy and its application in mental retardation. *American Journal of Mental Retardation*, *92*(5), 401–429.

Autism Little Learners. (n.d.). [Social Stories for school]. Accessed at https://autismlittlelearners.com/social-stories-for-school on November 25, 2024.

Ayres, A. J. (1972). *Sensory integration and learning disorders*. Western Psychological Services.

Banger, C. (2022, May 24). *The importance of learning communities for K–12 students* [Blog post]. Accessed at www.d2l.com/blog/importance-learning-communities-for-k-12-students on September 5, 2024.

Bansal, S. (2014). Children with learning disabilities: Teaching effective coping strategies. *The Primary Teacher*, *39*(3), 57–69.

Bates, V. C. (2023). Capital, class, status, and social reproduction in music education: A critical review. *Action, Criticism, and Theory for Music Education*, *22*(1), 54–82.

Berklee College of Music. (n.d.). *Our history*. Accessed at https://college.berklee.edu/BIAESN/history on April 7, 2025.

Bernard, R. (2016). Disciplinary discord: The implications of teacher training for K–12 music education. In J. H. Davis (Ed.), *Discourse and disjuncture between the arts and higher education* (pp. 53–73). Palgrave Macmillan. https://doi.org/10.1057/978-1-137-55243-3_3

Bernard, R. (Host). (2022a, September 1). Precious Perez (No. 8) [Audio podcast episode]. In *ABLE Voices Podcast*. Accessed at https://college.berklee.edu/BIAESN/able-voices-podcast on May 22, 2025.

Bernard, R. (Host). (2022b, November 1). Adrian Anantawan (No. 12) [Audio podcast episode]. In *ABLE Voices Podcast*. Accessed at https://college.berklee.edu/BIAESN/able-voices-podcast on May 22, 2025.

Bernard, R. (2023). Necessary for some, and helpful for all: Preparing music educators to reach every student. *ORFEU*, *8*(2), Article e01010.

Bernard, R. (Host). (2024a, February 1). Jennifer Msumba (No. 43) [Audio podcast episode]. In *ABLE Voices Podcast*. Accessed at https://college.berklee.edu/BIAESN/able-voices-podcast on June 4, 2025.

Bernard, R. (Host). (2024b, September 15). Jeremy Andrew Davis (No. 58) [Audio podcast episode]. In *ABLE Voices Podcast*. Accessed at https://college.berklee.edu/BIAESN/able-voices-podcast on May 22, 2025.

BevJohns. (n.d.). *About Beverley H. Johns*. Accessed at https://bevjohns.org/biography on April 7, 2025.

Binder, L. (2021). *Look again: Making friends with sensory processing disorder* [Master's thesis, Bank Street College of Education]. Educate. https://educate.bankstreet.edu/independent-studies/261

Blythe, T. (1998). *The teaching for understanding guide*. Jossey-Bass.

Bogatz, T. (Host). (2019, October 15). Art for all: Universal Design for Learning (No. 190) [Audio podcast episode]. In *Art Ed Radio*. Accessed at https://theartofeducation.edu/podcasts/art-for-all-universal-design-for-learning-ep-190 on July 18, 2024.

Bowell, P., & Heap, B. (2010). Drama is not a dirty word: Past achievements, present concerns, alternative futures. *Research in Drama Education: The Journal of Applied Theatre and Performance*, *15*(4), 579–592.

Brame, C. J. (n.d.). *Active learning*. Accessed at https://cft.vanderbilt.edu/wp-content/uploads/sites/59/Active-Learning.pdf on May 22, 2025.

Brock, M. E., Schaefer, J. M., & Seaman, R. L. (2020). Self-determination and agency for all: Supporting students with severe disabilities. *Theory Into Practice*, *59*(2), 162–171.

Brunelle, K., Abdulle, S., & Gorey, K. M. (2020). Anxiety and depression among socioeconomically vulnerable students with learning disabilities: Exploratory meta-analysis. *Child and Adolescent Social Work Journal*, *37*, 359–367.

Bureau of Labor Statistics. (2025, February 25). *Persons with a disability: Labor force characteristics—2024* (Publication No. USDL-25-0247) [News release]. U.S. Department of Labor. Accessed at www.bls.gov/news.release/pdf/disabl.pdf on May 14, 2025.

Burton, S. L. (2011). Perspective consciousness and cultural relevancy: Partnership considerations for the re-conceptualization of music teacher preparation. *Arts Education Policy Review*, *112*(3), 122–129.

Butay, B. M. (2023, December 13). Yes to assigned seating? *The Phoenix*. Accessed at https://fhsphoenix.org/yes-to-assigned-seating on May 22, 2025.

Butler School of Music. (n.d.). *Judith Jellison*. Accessed at https://music.utexas.edu/about/people/judith-jellison on April 7, 2025.

Byron, L. (2018). *Art for all: Planning for variability in the visual arts classroom*. CAST.

Capin, P., & Vaughn, S. (2017). Improving reading and social studies learning for secondary students with reading disabilities. *TEACHING Exceptional Children*, *49*(4), 249–261.

Carol Gray Social Stories. (n.d.). *About Carol*. Accessed at https://carolgraysocialstories.com/about-2/carol-gray on November 20, 2024.

Casale, J., Browne, T., Murray, I. V., & Gupta, G. (2025). *Physiology, vestibular system*. StatPearls.

Cassidy, S. (2004). Learning styles: An overview of theories, models, and measures. *Educational Psychology*, *24*(4), 419–444.

CAST. (2024). *Universal Design for Learning Guidelines version 3.0*. Accessed at https://udlguidelines.cast.org on September 1, 2024.

Castellano, C. (2005). *Making it work: Educating the blind/visually impaired student in the regular school.* Information Age Publishing.

Center for Autism and Related Disabilities. (n.d.). *Visual supports*. Accessed at https://card.ufl.edu/resources/visual-supports on May 31, 2024.

Centers for Disease Control and Prevention. (2025, January 31). *Data and statistics on children's mental health*. Accessed at www.cdc.gov/children-mental-health/data-research/?CDC_AAref_Val=www.cdc.gov/childrensmentalhealth/data.html on April 14, 2024.

Cheon, S. H., Reeve, J., & Vansteenkiste, M. (2020). When teachers learn how to provide classroom structure in an autonomy-supportive way: Benefits to teachers and their students. *Teaching and Teacher Education*, *90*, Article 103004. https://doi.org/10.1016/j.tate.2019.103004

Cleveland Clinic. (n.d.a). *Anxiety in children*. Accessed at https://my.clevelandclinic.org/health/diseases/anxiety-in-children on April 16, 2024.

Cleveland Clinic. (n.d.b). *Proprioception*. Accessed at https://my.clevelandclinic.org/health/articles/proprioception on April 10, 2025.

Coduti, W. A., Hayes, J. A., Locke, B. D., & Youn, S. J. (2016). Mental health and professional help-seeking among college students with disabilities. *Rehabilitation Psychology*, *61*(3), 288–296.

Collaborative for Leadership in Ayres Sensory Integration. (n.d.). *About CLASI*. Accessed at www.cl-asi.org/about-clasi on April 16, 2024.

Como, D. H., Goodfellow, M., Hudak, D., & Cermak, S. A. (2024). A scoping review: Social Stories supporting behavior change for individuals with autism. *Journal of Occupational Therapy, Schools, and Early Intervention*, *17*(1), 154–175.

Conway, C. (2020). *Teaching music in higher education* (2nd ed.). Oxford University Press.

Cowley Ford, A. (Host). (2023, December 18). Finnegan Shannon (No. 40) [Audio podcast episode]. In *ABLE Voices Podcast*. Accessed at https://college.berklee.edu/BIAESN/able-voices-podcast on May 22, 2025.

Cree, R. A., Okoro, C. A., Zack, M. M., & Carbone, E. (2018). Frequent mental distress among adults, by disability status, disability type, and selected characteristics—United States, 2018. *Morbidity and Mortality Weekly Report (MMWR)*, *69*(36), 1238–1243. http://dx.doi.org/10.15585/mmwr.mm6936a2

Cummins, R. A. (1991). Sensory integration and learning disabilities: Ayres' factor analyses reappraised. *Journal of Learning Disabilities, 24*(3), 160–168.

Cushman, C. (2024). *Tactile graphics* [Blog post]. Paths to Literacy. Accessed at www.pathstoliteracy.org/tactile-graphics on June 1, 2024.

Division of Visual and Performing Arts Education. (2023, September 20). *DARTS officers*. Accessed at https://darts.exceptionalchildren.org/darts-officers on April 7, 2025.

Dr. Alice Hammel. (n.d.). *Dr. Alice Hammel*. Accessed at https://alicehammel.com on April 7, 2025.

Early Learning Ventures. (n.d.). *Classroom layout guide*. Accessed at www.earlylearningventures.org/classroom-layout-guide on September 5, 2024.

Education for All Handicapped Children Act of 1975, 20 U.S.C. § 1401 (1975).

Edunators. (n.d.). *Previewing as a free and easy student intervention*. Accessed at www.edunators.com/articles/classroom-strategies/previewing-as-a-free-and-easy-student-intervention on November 18, 2024.

Everett, G. (Host). (2023, March 15). Grace Douglas (No. 21) [Audio podcast episode]. In *ABLE Voices Podcast*. Accessed at https://college.berklee.edu/BIAESN/able-voices-podcast on May 22, 2025.

Fallace, T. (2023). The long origins of the visual, auditory, and kinesthetic learning style typology, 1921–2001. *History of Psychology*, *26*(4), 334–354.

Fehr, R. (2015, April 8). *NAfME's history, the evolution of music education—and Taylor Swift!* [Blog post]. Accessed at https://nafme.org/blog/nafmes-history-the-evolution-of-music-education-and-taylor-swift on April 7, 2025.

Flannery, M. E. (2019, March). *The epidemic of anxiety among today's students*. NEA Today. Accessed at www.nea.org/nea-today/all-news-articles/epidemic-anxiety-among-todays-students on April 14, 2024.

Florida State University School of Music. (n.d.). *Faculty*. Accessed at www.liquidclay.com/com/darrow.htm on April 7, 2025.

Ford, J. W., Wenner, J. A., & Murphy, V. (2019). The effects of completing PREP Academy: A university-based transition project for students with disabilities (Practice brief). *Journal of Postsecondary Education and Disability*, *32*(1), 83–90.

Freire, P. (1970). *Pedagogy of the oppressed* (M. Bergman Ramos, Trans.). Herder and Herder. (Original work published 1968)

Furlonger, R., Garner, N., Callaghan, L., Foreman, S., & Bryson, C. (2020). Empowering students through partnership in the curriculum. In S. Mawani & A. A. Mukadam (Eds.), *Student empowerment in higher education: Reflecting on teaching practice and learner engagement* (Vol. 1, pp. 239–252). Logos Verlag Berlin.

Galiana-Simal, A., Vela-Romero, M., Romero-Vela, V. M., Oliver-Tercero, N., García-Olmo, V., Benito-Castellanos, P. J., et al. (2020). Sensory processing disorder: Key points of a frequent alteration in neurodevelopmental disorders. *Cogent Medicine*, *7*(1), Article 1736829.

Gardner, H. (1983). *Frames of mind: The theory of multiple intelligences*. Basic Books.

Gasiewski, K., & Weiss, M. J. (2022, August). *Sensory Integration theory and Ayres Sensory Integration* [Treatment summary]. Association for Science in Autism Treatment. Accessed at www.melmark.org/wp-content/uploads/2022/08/ASAT-Kristina-Gaisewski-Mary-Jane-Weiss-Sensory-Integration-Theory-2022.pdf on November 18, 2024.

Giroux, H. A. (1981). *Ideology, culture, and the process of schooling*. Temple University Press.

Gold, M. W. (1976). Task analysis of a complex assembly task by the retarded blind. *Exceptional Children*, *43*(2), 78–84.

Gordon, D. (Ed.). (2024). *Universal Design for Learning: Principles, framework, and practice* (Updated ed.). CAST.

Gray, C. A. (2010). *The new social story book* (Revised and expanded 10th anniversary ed.). Future Horizons.

Gray, C. A., Broek, E., Cain, S. L., Dutkiewicz, M., Fleck, C., Gray, B., et al. (Eds.). (1994). *The social story book*. Jenison Public Schools.

Gray, C. A., & Garand, J. D. (1993). Social Stories: Improving responses of students with autism with accurate social information. *Focus on Autistic Behavior*, *8*(1), 1–10.

Grumet, M. R. (1988). *Bitter milk: Women and teaching*. University of Massachusetts Press.

Harrington, A. B. (2018). *Using theater to promote the development of literacy and reading comprehension* [Master's thesis, Bank Street College of Education]. Educate. https://educate.bankstreet.edu/independent-studies/236

Hendrickson, J. M., Woods-Groves, S., Rodgers, D. B., & Datchuk, S. (2017). Perceptions of students with autism and their parents: The college experience. *Education and Treatment of Children*, *40*(4), 571–596.

Heumann, J. (2020). *Being Heumann: An unrepentant memoir of a disability rights activist*. Beacon Press.

Hodgdon, L. (2023). *Visual strategies for improving communication: Practical supports for autism spectrum disorders* (Updated and revised ed.). QuirkRoberts.

Hoehn, T. P., & Baumeister, A. A. (1994). A critique of the application of sensory integration therapy to children with learning disabilities. *Journal of Learning Disabilities*, *27*(6), 338–350.

Hourigan, R. (2007). Preparing music teachers to teach students with special needs. *Update: Applications of Research in Music Education*, *26*(1), 5–14.

Howard-Jones, P. A. (2014). Neuroscience and education: Myths and messages. *Nature Reviews Neuroscience*, *15*(12), 817–824.

Hyun, J., Ediger, R., & Lee, D. (2017). Students' satisfaction on their learning process in active learning and traditional classrooms. *International Journal of Teaching and Learning in Higher Education*, *29*(1), 108–118.

Individuals With Disabilities Education Act, 20 U.S.C. § 1400 (2004).

Iowa School of Music. (n.d.). *Mary Adamek*. Accessed at https://music.uiowa.edu/people/mary-adamek on April 7, 2025.

IRIS Center. (n.d.). *What can teachers do to improve their students' reading comprehension?* Accessed at https://iris.peabody.vanderbilt.edu/module/csr/cresource/q2/p05 on November 18, 2024.

Jacobs, J. (2023). Preparing the next generation of equity-centered teacher educators: Considerations for a pedagogy of teacher educator education. *Action in Teacher Education*, *45*(2), 159–181.

Jensen, A. P. (2008). Multimodal literacy and theater education. *Arts Education Policy Review*, *109*(5), 19–28.

Jiménez-Mijangos, L. P., Rodríguez-Arce, J., Martínez-Méndez, R., & Reyes-Lagos, J. J. (2023). Advances and challenges in the detection of academic stress and anxiety in the classroom: A literature review and recommendations. *Education and Information Technologies*, *28*(4), 3637–3666.

John F. Kennedy Presidential Library and Museum. (n.d.). *John F. Kennedy and people with intellectual disabilities*. Accessed at www.jfklibrary.org/learn/about-jfk/jfk-in-history/john-f-kennedy-and-people-with-intellectual-disabilities on April 7, 2025.

Jones, P. M. (2012). Key challenges to collegiate music education programs in North America. *Teachers College Record*, *114*(13), 93–111.

Kampwirth, T. J., & Bates, M. (1980). Modality preference and teaching method: A review of the research. *Academic Therapy*, *15*(5), 597–605.

Kennedy Center. (n.d.). *Access/VSA*. Accessed at www.kennedy-center.org/education/vsa on April 7, 2025.

Kent State University. (2022, December 9). *School of art*. Accessed at www.kent.edu/art/news/kent-state-university-faculty-juliann-dorff-named-ohio-art-educator-year on April 7, 2025.

Kidd, A. (n.d.). *From the student with anxiety* [Blog post]. Accessed at www.kcresolve.com/blog/from-the-student-with-anxiety on April 13, 2024.

Kiernan, L. (Producer). (1997). *Creating multiple paths for learning: Tape 1. Differentiating instruction* [Video program]. ASCD.

Kilroy, E., Aziz-Zadeh, L., & Cermak, S. (2019). Ayres theories of autism and sensory integration revisited: What contemporary neuroscience has to say. *Brain Sciences*, *9*(3), Article 68.

Kirschner, P. A. (2017). Stop propagating the learning styles myth. *Computers and Education*, *106*, 166–171.

Kojovic, N., Ben Hadid, L., Franchini, M., & Schaer, M. (2019). Sensory processing issues and their association with social difficulties in children with autism spectrum disorders. *Journal of Clinical Medicine*, *8*(10), Article 1508.

Kong, M., & Moreno, M. A. (2018). Sensory processing in children. *JAMA Pediatrics*, *172*(12), Article 1208.

Kosky Deskin, B. (2013, December 10). *A complete guide for using prompts to teach individuals with special needs* [Blog post]. Accessed at www.friendshipcircle.org/blog/2013/04/22/a-complete-guide-for-using-prompts-to-teach-individuals-with-special-needs on May 31, 2024.

Kratus, J. (2007). Music education at the tipping point. *Music Educators Journal*, *94*(2), 42–48.

Kratus, J. (2009, September 10–12). *Subverting the permanent curriculum in music education* [Paper presentation]. 2009 Symposium on Music Teacher Education, Greensboro, North Carolina, United States.

Kratus, J. (2011, February 2–5). *The role of personal expressiveness in the formation of identity among beginning songwriters* [Paper presentation]. Suncoast Music Education Research Symposium, Tampa, Florida, United States.

Kratus, J. (2015). The role of subversion in changing music education. In C. Randles (Ed.), *Music education: Navigating the future* (pp. 340–346). Routledge.

Kulkarni, S. S., Miller, A. L., Nusbaum, E. A., Pearson, H., & Brown, L. X. Z. (2024). Toward disability-centered, culturally sustaining pedagogies in teacher education. *Critical Studies in Education*, *65*(2), 107–127.

Ladau, E. (2021). *Demystifying disability: What to know, what to say, and how to be an ally*. Ten Speed Press.

Lane, S. J., Mailloux, Z., Schoen, S., Bundy, A., May-Benson, T. A., Parham, L. D., et al. (2019). Neural foundations of Ayres Sensory Integration. *Brain Sciences*, *9*(7), 153.

Leaf, J. B., Ferguson, J. L., Cihon, J. H., Milne, C. M., Leaf, R., & McEachin, J. (2020). A critical review of social narratives. *Journal of Developmental and Physical Disabilities*, *32*(2), 241–256.

Lewis, V. (2024, August). *High contrast and low vision*. Accessed at www.perkins.org/resource/choosing-high-contrast-color-schemes-for-low-vision on June 1, 2024.

Lexia. (2023, April 13). *Best reading strategies for special education students* [Blog post]. Accessed at www.lexialearning.com/blog/best-reading-strategies-for-special-education-students on November 20, 2024.

Luther, M. (2023, August 1). *The case for assigned seats*. Accessed at https://thebrokencopier.substack.com/p/the-case-for-assigned-seats on November 18, 2024.

Maternal and Child Health and Mental Retardation Planning Amendments of 1963, Pub. L. No. 88-156, 77 Stat. 273 (1963).

Mathew, D. (2015). *Fragile learning: The influence of anxiety*. Routledge.

Mathew, D. (2016). *Fragile learning* [Doctoral dissertation, University of Bedfordshire]. Open Repository. https://uobrep.openrepository.com/handle/10547/622106

McConomy, M. A., Root, J., & Wade, T. (2022). Using task analysis to support inclusion and assessment in the classroom. *TEACHING Exceptional Children*, *54*(6), 414–422.

McLaren, P. (1989). *Life in schools: An introduction to critical pedagogy in the foundations of education*. Longman.

McVay, P., Wilson, H., & Chiotti, L. (2003). "I see what you mean!" Examples of visual tools to promote inclusive learning. *Disability Solutions*, *5*(5), 1, 13.

Means, B. (1993). Cognitive task analysis as a basis for instructional design. In M. Rabinowitz (Ed.), *Cognitive science foundations of instruction* (pp. 97–118). Routledge.

Melani, N. A., Mulyadi, M., & Firdaus, M. (2024). The influence of previewing predicting strategy and reading motivation toward seventh grade students' reading comprehension at Junior High School 10 of Palembang. *PPSDP International Journal of Education*, *3*(1), 188–194.

Miller, L. J. (2014). *Sensational kids: Hope and help for children with sensory processing disorder (SPD)* (Revised ed.). Perigee.

Miller, L. J., Schoen, S. A., Mulligan, S., & Sullivan, J. (2017). Identification of sensory processing and integration symptom clusters: A preliminary study. *Occupational Therapy International, 2017*, Article 2876080. https://doi.org/10.1155/2017/2876080

Moore College of Art and Design. (2019, October 1). *Moore hosts 2nd International Disability Studies, Arts & Education conference*. Accessed at https://moore.edu/news/moore-hosts-2nd-international-disability-studies-arts-education-conference on April 7, 2025.

Moyer, J. R., & Dardig, J. C. (1978). Practical task analysis for special educators. *TEACHING Exceptional Children*, *11*(1), 16–18.

Mustaniemi-Laakso, M., Katsui, H., & Heikkilä, M. (2023). Vulnerability, disability, and agency: Exploring structures for inclusive decision-making and participation in a responsive state. *International Journal for the Semiotics of Law*, *36*(4), 1581–1609.

National Art Education Association. (2024, May 2). *Art in special education (ASE)*. Accessed at www.arteducators.org/community/articles/75-art-in-special-education-ase on April 7, 2025.

NYU Steinhardt. (n.d.). *Elise Sobol*. Accessed at https://steinhardt.nyu.edu/people/elise-sobol on April 7, 2025.

Omairi, C., Mailloux, Z., Antoniuk, S. A., & Schaaf, R. (2022). Occupational therapy using Ayres Sensory Integration: A randomized controlled trial in Brazil. *American Journal of Occupational Therapy*, *76*(4), Article 7604205160.

Open Access. (n.d.). [CAST and the UDL Guidelines]. Accessed at www.openaccess-ca.org/cast-and-the-udl-guidelines on May 22, 2025.

Orkwis, R., & McLane, K. (1998). *A curriculum every student can use: Design principles for student access* (Publication No. ED 423 654) [Topical brief]. ERIC Clearinghouse on Disabilities and Gifted Education. Accessed at https://files.eric.ed.gov/fulltext/ED423654.pdf on May 27, 2025.

Palmer, A. J., & de Quadros, A. (Eds.). (2012). *Tanglewood II: Summoning the future of music education*. GIA.

Pape, B. (2018). *Learner variability is the rule, not the exception*. Digital Promise Global. Accessed at http://hdl.handle.net/20.500.12265/16 on April 14, 2024.

Paris, D., & Alim, H. S. (Eds.). (2017). *Culturally sustaining pedagogies: Teaching and learning for justice in a changing world*. Teachers College Press.

Pashler, H., McDaniel, M., Rohrer, D., & Bjork, R. (2009). Learning styles: Concepts and evidence. *Psychological Science in the Public Interest*, *9*(3), 105–119.

Perez, P. (Host). (2022, October 1). Shane Lowe (No. 10) [Audio podcast episode]. In *ABLE Voices Podcast*. Accessed at https://college.berklee.edu/BIAESN/able-voices-podcast on May 27, 2025.

Perkins School for the Blind. (n.d.). *General tips for teaching science to students with visual impairments*. Accessed at www.perkins.org/resource/getting-started on June 1, 2024.

Pinar, W. F., & Grumet, M. R. (1976). *Toward a poor curriculum*. Kendall/Hunt.

Positive Action. (2025, March 20). *9 effective teaching strategies for students with emotional and behavioral disorders* [Blog post]. Accessed at www.positiveaction.net/blog/teaching-strategies-for-emotional-and-behavioral-disorders on June 2, 2024.

Pratt, C., & Steward, L. (2020). *Applied behavior analysis: The role of task analysis and chaining*. Accessed at www.iidc.indiana.edu/irca/articles/applied-behavior-analysis.html on November 20, 2024.

Randles, C. (Ed.). (2015). *Music education: Navigating the future*. Routledge.

Rehabilitation Act of 1973, 29 U.S.C. § 701 (1973).

Rehabilitation Act of 1973, 29 U.S.C. § 794 (1973).

Richards, R. G. (n.d.). *Helping children with learning disabilities understand what they read*. Accessed at www.ldonline.org/ld-topics/reading-dyslexia/helping-children-learning-disabilities-understand-what-they-read on November 20, 2024.

Rohrer, M., & Samson, N. (2014). *10 critical components for success in the special education classroom*. Corwin Press.

Rose, D. H., & Meyer, A. (Eds.). (2006). *A practical reader in Universal Design for Learning*. Harvard Education Press.

Rosenfeld, R. A. (1978). Anxiety and learning. *Teaching Sociology*, *5*(2), 151–166.

Sam, A., & Autism Focused Intervention Resources and Modules. (2016a). *Task analysis (TA): EBP brief packet*. National Professional Development Center on Autism Spectrum Disorder. Accessed at https://files.eric.ed.gov/fulltext/ED595409.pdf on May 27, 2025.

Sam, A., & Autism Focused Intervention Resources and Modules. (2016b). *Visual support (VS): EBP brief packet*. National Professional Development Center on Autism Spectrum Disorder. Accessed at https://files.eric.ed.gov/fulltext/ED595398.pdf on May 27, 2025.

Schaaf, R. C., & Mailloux, Z. (2015). *Clinician's guide for implementing Ayres Sensory Integration: Promoting participation for children with autism*. AOTA Press.

SkyCare ABA. (n.d.). *Task analysis in ABA: An overview* [Blog post]. Accessed at https://skycareaba.com/blogs-task-analysis-in-aba-an-overview on November 18, 2024.

Social Security Act, 42 U.S.C. §§ 301-1307 (1940).

Stahl, S. A. (1999, Fall). Different strokes for different folks? A critique of learning styles. *American Educator*, *23*(3), 27–31.

Steinbrenner, J. R., Hume, K., Odom, S. L., Morin, K. L., Nowell, S. W., Tomaszewski, B., et al. (2020). *Evidence-based practices for children, youth, and young adults with autism spectrum disorder.* Frank Porter Graham Child Development Institute.

Student Disability Services. (n.d.). *Tips for teaching students who are blind or visually impaired*. Accessed at www.utsa.edu/disability/faculty-staff/tips-teaching-blind.html on June 1, 2024.

Syeda, M. M., & Andrews, J. J. W. (2015). Supporting students with anxiety in schools. *The Inclusive Educator Journal*, *1*(1), 29–36.

Tactile Graphics. (n.d.). *Introduction to tactile graphics: A basic overview*. Accessed at www.tactilegraphics.org/whataretgs.html on June 1, 2024.

Teschers, C., Neuhaus, T., & Vogt, M. (2024). Troubling the boundaries of traditional schooling for a rapidly changing future—Looking back and looking forward. *Educational Philosophy and Theory*, *56*(9), 873–884.

Toivanen, T., Mikkola, K., & Ruismäki, H. (2012). The challenge of an empty space: Pedagogical and multimodal interaction in drama lessons. *Procedia: Social and Behavioral Sciences*, *69*, 2082–2091.

Tomlinson, C. A. (1995). *How to differentiate instruction in mixed-ability classrooms*. ASCD.

Tomlinson, C. A. (1997). *Creating multiple paths for learning.* Video interview by Leslie Kiernan.

Tomlinson, C. A. (2014). *The differentiated classroom: Responding to the needs of all learners* (2nd ed.). ASCD.

Tomlinson, C. A. (2017). *How to differentiate instruction in academically diverse classrooms* (3rd ed.). ASCD.

Ukrainetz, T. A. (2016). Strategic intervention for expository texts: Teaching text preview and lookback. *Perspectives of the ASHA Special Interest Groups*, *1*(1), 99–108.

U.S. Department of Education. (n.d.). *Frequently asked questions: Section 504 free appropriate public education (FAPE)*. Accessed at www.ed.gov/laws-and-policy/civil-rights-laws/disability-discrimination/frequently-asked-questions-section-504-fape on April 7, 2025.

U.S. Department of Education. (2024, February 16). *A history of the Individuals With Disabilities Education Act*. Accessed at https://sites.ed.gov/idea/IDEA-History on April 7, 2025.

U.S. Department of Labor. (n.d.). *Section 504, Rehabilitation Act of 1973*. Accessed at www.dol.gov/agencies/oasam/centers-offices/civil-rights-center/statutes/section-504-rehabilitation-act-of-1973 on April 11, 2025.

Valentine, K. (Host). (2024, July 1). Rae Brazill (No. 53) [Audio podcast episode]. In *ABLE Voices Podcast*. Accessed at https://college.berklee.edu/BIAESN/able-voices-podcast on May 27, 2025.

Wang, Z., Whiteside, S., Sim, L., Farah, W., Morrow, A., Alsawas, M., et al. (2017, August). *Anxiety in children* (Comparative Effectiveness Review, No. 192; AHRQ Publication No. 17-EHC023-EF) [Report]. Agency for Healthcare Research and Quality. Accessed at www.ncbi.nlm.nih.gov/sites/books/NBK476277/pdf/Bookshelf_NBK476277.pdf on May 27, 2025.

Watling, R., & Hauer, S. (2015). Effectiveness of Ayres Sensory Integration and sensory-based interventions for people with autism spectrum disorder: A systematic review. *The American Journal of Occupational Therapy*, *69*(5), Article 6905180030.

West, J. E., McLaughlin, V. L., Shepherd, K. G., & Cokley, R. (2023). The Americans With Disabilities Act and the Individuals With Disabilities Education Act: Intersection, divergence, and the path forward. *Journal of Disability Policy Studies*, *34*(3), 224–234.

Whiting, C. C., Schoen, S. A., & Niemeyer, L. (2023). A sensory integration intervention in the school setting to support performance and participation: A multiple-baseline study. *The American Journal of Occupational Therapy*, *77*(2), Article 7702205060.

Willingham, D. T., Hughes, E. M., & Dobolyi, D. G. (2015). The scientific status of learning styles theories. *Teaching of Psychology*, *42*(3), 266–271.

Willings, C. (n.d.). *Font legibility*. Accessed at www.teachingvisuallyimpaired.com/font-legibility.html on June 1, 2024.

Wininger, S. R., Redifer, J. L., Norman, A. D., & Ryle, M. K. (2019). Prevalence of learning styles in educational psychology and introduction to education textbooks: A content analysis. *Psychology Learning and Teaching*, *18*(3), 221–243.

Wong, A. (Ed.). (2020). *Disability visibility: First-person stories from the twenty-first century*. Vintage Books.

Wooldridge, S. (2023, April 12). *Writing respectfully: Person-first and identity-first language*. Accessed at www.nih.gov/about-nih/what-we-do/science-health-public-trust/perspectives/writing-respectfully-person-first-identity-first-language on October 12, 2024.

Wyss, C., Kocher, M., & Baer, M. (2017). The dilemma of dealing with persistent teaching traditions: Findings of a video study. *Journal of Education for Teaching*, *43*(2), 191–205.

INDEX

A

B

C

D

E

F

G

H

I

N

O

P

Q

R

S

T

Honoring Each Learner
Keely Keller
Author Keely Keller presents a five-step process to help teachers individualize learning. By assessing strengths, addressing challenges, and creating unique learning plans, educators can personalize instruction, create equity, and build inclusive classrooms that ensure every student thrives.
BKG265

The General Education Teacher's Guide to Autism
Barbara Boroson
In this engaging title, you will find answers to all your questions about students on the autism spectrum in inclusive classrooms. Collect the information and strategies you need to create an effective, welcoming, and supportive environment for these neurodivergent students.
BKG055

All Means All
Heather Friziellie, Julie A. Schmidt, and Jeanne Spiller
Discover practical strategies to implement an inclusive philosophy through collaborative teamwork and shared ownership of student learning. This book provides a framework for standards-based instruction, tailored teaching, progress monitoring, and targeted interventions, ultimately promoting equitable learning opportunities for all students.
BKG119

The New Art and Science of Teaching Art and Music
Mark Onuscheck, Robert J. Marzano, and Jonathan Grice
Built on the foundation of the New Art and Science of Teaching framework, this research-based resource outlines an art- and music-specific model of instruction. Rely on the book's myriad strategies to enhance your daily practice and promote the creative potential and critical thinking skills of every student.
BKF817

Solution Tree | Press 

Visit SolutionTree.com or call 800.733.6786 to order.

We don't just help schools make a change, we help them *be* **the change**

REAL IMPACT. RELEVANT SOLUTIONS. RESULTS-DRIVEN APPROACH.

From funding to faculty retention, the evolving demands schools face can be overwhelming. That's where we come in. With professional development rooted in decades of research and delivered by many of the educators who literally wrote the book on it, we empower schools to achieve meaningful change with real, sustainable results.

The change starts here. We can make it happen together.

See how we can get real results for your school or district.

Scan the code or visit:

SolutionTree.com/Results-Driven

Solution Tree

LET'S SEE WHAT **WE CAN** DO TOGETHER